LUCRETIUS

SELECTIONS FROM THE
DE RERUM NATURA

In Memoriam Les Spink (1922-1998)

LUCRETIUS

SELECTIONS FROM THE
DE RERUM NATURA

Edited with Introduction
and Commentary by

John Godwin

Bristol Classical Press

First published in 2000
Bristol Classical Press
an imprint of
Gerald Duckworth & Co. Ltd
61 Frith Street
London W1V 5TA
e-mail: inquiries@duckworth-publishers.co.uk
Website: www.ducknet.co.uk

A catalogue record for this book is available
from the British Library

ISBN 1-85399-486-3

Printed in Great Britain by
Booksprint

CONTENTS

PREFACE

Lucretius was an ambitious poet. He aimed to recreate the Greek philosophy of Epicurus in Latin verse, to compose an original epic poem on a large scale and (as if that were not enough) to change the way we live our lives. The daunting task facing any edition of this poetry is to try to do justice to the several aspects of the poet's output and to explain the poetry and the philosophy to readers who may be unfamiliar with both. Above all, it is the job of the editor to try to bring out the sheer pleasure which can be had in reading this poet – who manages to be cerebral and sensual in equal proportions. This edition is aimed at the reader new to the work who wishes to read a few passages to see what this poetry is like. My hope is that at least some readers will be left dissatisfied at the end of the book and will seek out and read the whole poem for themselves.

In preparing this edition I have been greatly helped by many people. Chris Emlyn-Jones supervised my Ph.D. thesis on Lucretius and made me re-evaluate many of my cosy assumptions about this most provocative of poets: David Sedley read the Introduction and made many acute observations; the entire manuscript was read by Desmond Costa, Leofranc Holford-Strevens, Matthew Leigh and Martin Thorpe with astonishing generosity of effort, time and spirit. I learned enormously from their remarks and only hope that the final product will do them justice. Those mistakes which remain are, of course, my own.

John Godwin
Shrewsbury
September 1999

INTRODUCTION

The life of Lucretius

As with many ancient poets, our information about the life of Lucretius is scanty in the extreme. We do not possess an ancient *Life* of this poet as we do for the poets Virgil and Horace, and the nearest thing to a biography which survives is the pithy thumbnail sketch of St Jerome, who records the following as having occurred in the year 94 BC:

> The poet Titus Lucretius Carus was born. A love potion drove him mad, and he composed, in the intervals of his insanity, several books which Cicero corrected. He committed suicide aged 43.

The testimony of Jerome is regarded with extreme scepticism by most scholars. For one thing, it appears to be a salvo of moral condemnation from a Christian against a poet who inveighed against religion, for another it makes a mockery of Virgil's praise of Lucretius as a 'happy man' (*Georgics* 2.490-2): '*felix qui potuit rerum cognoscere causas*'. It would be insensitive in the extreme for Virgil to have written in such terms about a man who had committed suicide in such unhappy circumstances. There is a stray reference in a letter of Cicero to his brother (*ad Quintum fratrem* 1.10.3) composed in February 54 BC: 'The lines of Lucretius contain, as you say in your letter, many flashes of inspiration but also much poetic skill'; *multis luminibus ingenii, multae tamen artis* is a typically sharp summary of the flavour of this poet – and the date of the letter demonstrates that the poem was in circulation by 54. For the social background and the life of the poet we have no information outside the poem itself. An attempt has been made (Wiseman [1974]) to produce an analysis of the poet's life and interests from the poetry, but this sort of documentary treatment of poetry is fraught with problems: we cannot be sure that this is not misreading the poet's attempts to capture the interests of his potential audience as evidence of his own lifestyle.

Epicurus and his Philosophy

Lucretius' poem expounds the philosophy of Epicurus (341-270 BC). Greek philosophers had long been investigating the nature of the world before Epicurus. The philosophers before Socrates (the Presocratics) had speculated on whether the world consisted of one element (earth, air, fire, or water) or else a mixture of elements: then the fifth-century thinkers Democritus and Leucippus came up with the atomic theory which has dominated scientific understanding of the nature of matter – at least until atoms proved *not* to be indivisible after all. Epicurus took over and developed this explanation of the nature of the universe and formed a full philosophy of life from it.

In its simplest form, the theory starts from the familiar principle of conservation of matter which asserts simply that nothing can be made from nothing (1.150): Epicurus further states that there is only matter and empty space in the universe and that this matter is made up of indivisible atoms (the Greek word *atomos* means 'uncuttable') which are too small for the eye to see but whose existence can be inferred in theory from the continued existence of things – for if matter could be subdivided to an infinite extent then (in an infinity of time) all things would have disintegrated to nothing by now (1.540-550). Everything is the result of atomic confluence: and death is the disintegration of the atomic *concilium* which is a human being, allowing the atoms (which are indestructible) to form other *concilia*. There must be empty space for the atoms to move in – and also to explain the different weights and densities of different sorts of object, so that a lump of lead has more atoms and less space than a lump of wood and so is heavier. This empty space is infinite – for what limit can there be to nothingness? – and hence the universe is infinite. The number of different atomic shapes and sizes is finite – otherwise some would be big enough to be visible – but the number of individual atoms of each size and shape is infinite. The atoms are all made of the same sort of matter, but they vary in size and shape and this variety produces the variety in the world of visible phenomena.

These atoms are always moving and colliding to form material compounds. Gravity makes things fall and so one would expect the atoms all to fall downwards in the same direction, like raindrops. This however would not allow the atoms to collide sufficiently to form *concilia* and so must be wrong, the logic being that if there were no swerve then there would be no *concilia*; but *concilia* do exist – and so there must be a swerve. One might equally have thought that the heavier atoms would fall faster than the lighter ones and land on top of them (forming vertical *concilia*) but Epicurus asserted that all atoms fall at the same speed and then invented the theory of the 'swerve' (*parenklisis* in Epicurus' Greek, *clinamen* in Latin) which states that atoms veer from the downward path on occasion and bang into each other, causing a ricochet of atoms which injects horizontal movement into the otherwise vertical stream. This is highly dubious as an argument and ignores other possibilities, but it does provide an imperfect solution to his dilemma. It also has the virtue of adding an element of uncertainty into a mechanical universe and thus helps to account for free-will and volition.

Epicurus took over a great deal of the thinking of the fifth-century Democritus but reproached his predecessor with leaving no alternative to inexorable causation and thus no room for human free will. If, indeed, we are atomic *concilia* like the humblest brick, and if all *concilia* obey the laws of cause and effect, then it is difficult to see how one could explain the feeling of free human choice. Looked at another way, we are the product of random atomic movement in an infinite universe where no gods tend to us and so if everything is random, even including our sense of free will and voluntary movements, then the notion of volition is an illusion. This would furthermore have denied the possibility of any 'conversion' to Epicureanism: if I have no free will then I can no more change my way of life than my car can mend its own puncture. Epicurus and Lucretius, however, argued that we do in fact have the power to move and change ourselves; and they sought to explain this in atomic terms of the swerve and also as part of their account of perception and thought (4.722-1036).

Epicurus explained perception as the result of atomic contact between material objects and our sense-organs. This is obvious in the case of touch and taste, and credible in the case of smell and hearing, but it is more difficult to sustain when discussing sight. Here the Epicurean theory is that fine 'images' are constantly leaving the surfaces of things and entering our eyes – although it does not explain, for example, how the elephantine image of an elephant could enter my tiny eye-sockets. Epicurus famously asserted that 'all perceptions are true'. This is provocative since we see things in dreams which are obviously not 'really' there, and optical illusions had already convinced sceptics to doubt the reliability of at least some of our empirical experience. We see an oar partly submerged in water which 'looks' bent but turns out to be straight when pulled out of the river (4.436-42). The tower which is in fact square looks round at a distance (4.353-63). Epicurus asserted here that our senses are in fact reporting correctly – as the 'image' from the square tower will have its angles eroded in flying through the air and be 'rounded' off by the time it reaches our eyes. He also postulated that often the fault lies with our minds' 'addition of opinion' which jumps to the conclusion that just because the *image* looks round the object itself is round. Images come into the mind unsorted, leaving the mind to explain and interpret them, which effectively gets Epicurus off the sceptics' hook as he can always say that the mind is mistaken in believing that the 'bent' oar is 'really' bent just because the *image* is 'bent' – the perception is 'true' but used falsely by the mind.

Book Four of the poem begins as an exercise in refuting the 'proof' of life after death from the existence of ghosts – but the chief enemy faced in the book is not the spiritualist but the sceptic. The sceptics refused to accept the validity of sense-experience: if some such experience (e.g. dreams) is clearly wrong, then how do we know that it is not all wrong? Diogenes Laertius (9.62) in his life of the sceptic Pyrrho reported how Pyrrho 'faced all risks – traffic, precipices, dogs' and was saved from harm only by his less sceptical friends who would pull him out of the path of oncoming traffic. There was plenty of scepticism in the atomist tradition: Democritus said that 'in reality we know nothing' (frag. 117 KRS) and Epicurus' teacher Nausiphanes was also attracted to Pyrrho's scepticism (Diogenes Laertius 9.64). The Academy of Plato was 'converted' to scepticism when Arcesilaus of Pitane became its head. The greatest statement of the sceptic position was found in Aenesidemus (1st century BC, although we do not know whether his work was known to Lucretius) who probably originated the famous 'Ten Modes of Scepticism', and then in Sextus Empiricus (2nd century AD, on whom see Annas and Barnes). The refutation of scepticism occupies Lucretius a great deal: after all, if we cannot be certain that we are perceiving the truth, then it will be difficult to be sure that we can make sensible judgements about the nature of the universe.

Epicurus believed in the gods – since they are seen in visions there must be something there – but (like many people throughout the ages) he made the gods reflect his notion of the good life. His gods were models of serenity, living in a cloudless, windless paradise of detached contentment (3.18-24) in the gaps between the worlds (which Cicero called the *intermundia*, translating Epicurus' *metakosmia*) and their bodies are as deathless as the atoms of which all bodies are composed. By this token, however, they cannot be involved in the life of men, on the syllogistic reasoning that:

The gods enjoy a life free of all cares
If they cared about us they would not enjoy a life free of care
Therefore they do not care about us.

This means that the whole apparatus of personal and public religion is a waste of time if it seeks to acquire favours from unheeding gods, and Lucretius mocks the practice of sacrifice (1.80-101) and prayers to render the impotent man fertile (4.1236-9): the impotent man needs *semen* and not the *numen* of the gods, he remarks wittily. Epicurus' gods are not the bullying beings of myth who fling thunderbolts to punish us (and end up hitting their own temples (6.387-422)). There is scope for 'prayer' although it is not communication with the gods but rather contemplation of their divine nature and meditation on their peaceful serenity. We ourselves can live a life worthy of the gods if we follow their examples and banish fear and anxiety, using them as role-models rather than divine Godfathers to be placated and entreated. Epicurus managed this sort of felicity to such an extent that he deserves to be called a god (5.8).

All this is a fascinating chapter in the history of science and philosophy, no doubt, but it does not explain why anyone should get excited about atoms. It is hard to see why people should surrender the colourful gods of myth for these faceless, idle bon viveurs, especially since the removal of the gods also removes one possible hope of manipulating nature and leaves us totally at the mercy of the random devastation of atomic collisions – as is brought out only too well in the section on the plague (6.1138-1286). Why should this philosophy of atomic mechanisms appeal to the general public at all? To understand this we need to see Epicurus' moral and social philosophy in the context of late-republican Rome.

Morality for Epicurus is a matter of what is best for us both as individuals and as a society. The greatest good is in fact pleasure, and Epicureans soon acquired a reputation for being hedonistic 'epicures' addicted to a life of gluttony, debauchery and luxurious indulgence which is far from being an accurate picture of their real beliefs. In fact Epicurus saw pleasure as being the removal of want and pain so that our satisfaction in, say, eating is proportionate to our hunger and such that once the pain of want has been removed the enjoyment cannot be increased but only varied. He divided pleasures up into the two categories: kinetic and katastematic. Kinetic pleasure involves movement of the sense-organs in such things as the ingestion of food or the ejaculation of sperm, while katastematic pleasure is the static equilibrium of not needing anything, the highest state of which is the Epicurean ideal of *ataraxia* ('not being disturbed'). Kinetic pleasures arise from satisfying three kinds of desires:

1) natural and necessary (e.g. food and drink)
2) natural but not necessary (e.g. sex)
3) unnatural and unnecessary (luxuries).

The wise man will indulge the first sort as he needs, the second sort with the greatest caution and the third sort not at all. A passage such as 2.20-36, with its constant satire of the expensive luxury which is no better than freely available goods, is typical of the Epicurean attitude towards pleasure whereby the wise man will train himself to be content with a little (the famous *paruum quod satis est* as at 5.1119) so that he will always be content: this produces an austere philosophy far removed from the 'epicure'. The man addicted to satisfying unnecessary desires is a fool – or one tormented like the daughters of Danaus in Lucretius' remythologising of the Underworld (3.1003-10). If we develop our tastes so that, for example, bread will no longer suffice but we must have caviar, then we have not increased our pleasure but merely increased the possibility of pain. Similarly, the romantic attachment to one lover will produce frustration when that lover is unavailable or unwilling, and so Lucretius recommends promiscuity (4.1065-6) as better calculated to free us from pain. What goes for the body also goes for the mind: greed for power and money is also unnecessary and insatiable and the wise man will eliminate this labour of Sisyphus (3.995-1002) altogether. This leaves Epicurus with the paradox that 'poverty is the greatest wealth and unlimited wealth is great poverty' (*Vatican Sayings* 25): or as Lucretius puts it:

> If a man guides his life by true philosophy he will find ample riches in a modest livelihood enjoyed with a tranquil mind. Of that little he need never be beggared. (5.1117-9)

This raises questions about the social duty of the wise man: traditional Epicureanism seems to espouse a selfish dedication to personal pleasure and freedom from attachment which would seem to make all social commitment impossible. The wise man will retreat into his garden, live unobtrusively and avoid any contact with his fellow-men that does not further his own pleasure – which all sounds rather self-centred.

Over against this bleak view of Epicureanism is the master's insistence on the importance of friendship. This is not innate in man – early man was (he says) a lone wolf who only came together with others when it dawned on him that there was greater safety in numbers – but became the overriding ethical good for the wise man:

> Of all the things that wisdom acquires for the blessedness of life, the greatest by far is the possession of friendship.
>
> (Epicurus, *Key Doctrines* 27)

Such friendship marked the advance of man from his earlier bestial state:

> Epicurus said that you should be more concerned at inspecting with whom you are eating and drinking than what you eat and drink. For feeding without a friend is the life of a lion and a wolf.
>
> (Seneca, *Letters* 19.10)

Friendship, then, is the overriding social virtue for mankind and may in turn also bring other social benefits such as justice and compassion. It will not, in itself, however, deliver political commitment, and Epicurus was also famed for his antipolitical stance (see Fowler). The 'friends' in his circle are fellow-Epicureans and the Garden was open only to the sympathisers and not to the unenlightened rabble. Contact with the rest of humanity might convert people and thus produce more serenity in the world to enjoy, and one Epicurean (Diogenes of Oenoanda NF 21) dreams of a world totally converted to Epicureanism. The reality was of course very different: this world has never been the paradise of enlightenment that Epicurus would have liked, and certainly not the Roman world of Lucretius' era and the years which followed his death.

In the 80's BC the dictator Sulla had taken over the city of Rome and massacred large numbers of citizens, and after his death the political life of the capital became increasingly dominated by corruption and cruelty as competing army-commanders sought to seize the power which Sulla had so ruthlessly enjoyed, while on the streets the demagogues such as Clodius found popular success a route to popular power. Civil war in 49 BC ended with Pompey butchered and Caesar in charge of the Roman state – a dictatorship from which Caesar's assassination, in 44, gave only brief respite before plunging Rome back into civil strife for a dozen years until Caesar's heir, Octavian, finally defeated Caesar's consul, Mark Antony, at the battle of Actium and set himself up as the ruler of Rome. Throughout the hundred or so years from 133 to 27 the citizen had less and less say in the running of the republic as an individual but considerable force as a member of a mob; and by the lifetime of Lucretius even the old nobility who had formerly dominated the senate found themselves marginalised by the power of the competing army commanders. If ever there was a society susceptible to the appeal of the apolitical tranquillity of the Epicurean garden, it was this Rome where the streets ran with blood and where politics was becoming either a tragedy or a farce.

The *de rerum natura*

The genre to which this poem belongs is the didactic epic: a branch of epic poetry whose purpose is to instruct the reader with knowledge of the world. The first ancient practitioner of the genre was the eighth-century Greek poet Hesiod, whose works *Theogony* (concerning the birth of the gods) and *Works and Days* (advice to the poet's brother Perses about farming and related matters) still survive. After Hesiod there are texts by philosophers such as Parmenides and Empedocles, and then a great deal more when the literary capital of the world moved from Greece to Egypt and the great cultural centre of Alexandria.

Here was a library of world-historical importance, staffed and used by men of colossal intelligence and literary interest such as Callimachus, Apollonius, Theocritus. Here, more than anywhere else in the world, a didactic poet could find all the information he wanted, transfer it to verse, and demonstrate both his mastery of arcane information and his dexterity in reproducing this knowledge in verse of dazzling ingenuity and lucidity. Here was born the metaphrast: the poet who responds to the ultimate artistic challenge of producing poetry out of rather dull factual information and thus creates *tours de force* such as Nicander of Colophon's *Venomous Reptiles* and *Antidotes to Poisons*, works designed to be admired and enjoyed by a literary audience rather than being aimed at the wary hill-walker. It is not that the information contained in such poetry is not correct – the prose manuals which the poet consulted were generally the best available – but that there is a chasm between the people *about* whom the poet was writing and the audience *for* whom he composed. The old notion of Nicander being consulted by the Alexandrian Ramblers' Association dies hard, but all that we know about this sort of poetry assures us that it was the entertainment of the salon rather than the handbook of the hills.

In Rome we have evidence of didactic poetry being written in Lucretius' own day. Cicero himself translated Aratus' *Phainomena* into Latin, and we know of a (lost) poem called *de rerum natura* being written by an Egnatius, while a certain Sallustius wrote an *Empedoclea*. This is all, it has often been said, simply poets looking for something to write about.

Similar things might be said about Virgil's *Georgics*: a didactic poem in four books composed after Lucretius' death between 37 and 30 BC and concerned to expound the techniques of farming. The poem shows enormous poetic and literary skill and a good deal of enthusiasm for the subject and for the land of Italy, but alas hardly any evidence of first-hand knowledge of farming on the part of the poet. It may be disillusioning to realise that all the information contained in the *Georgics* could have been conned from, say, the prose *de re rustica* of Virgil's contemporary Varro. To feel that this line of argument undermines the poem would be a mistake, however. Long gone are the days when poetry was seen as a document of real life whose ostensible 'meaning' was obviously its 'purpose'. Virgil composed a poem about farming which possesses a beauty and a wonder which continue to astonish the reader: such beauty and wonder is not compromised by the question of whether the poet actually had a farm.

These questions are still central to much discussion of Lucretius, however, and the debate about this poem still ranges around the polar opposition between those who regard him as a missionary, preaching the good news of Epicurus with a view to converting the reader, and those who regard him as a metaphrast, picking up the challenge to compose Latin verses on the subject of atomic physics. On the one hand, the poet does claim to be aiming at the conversion of the addressee to the way of life espoused by Epicurus, and yet on the other hand there are many ways in which this does not seem to be the case. The vast majority of the text is concerned with scientific details of atomic physics, branching out into such arcane matters as the magnet, the waterspout, the question of the infinity of the universe and finite number of atomic shapes. Little of this (it might be argued) is much use in telling us how to live, and much of it reads like the metaphrast rather than the missionary, creating coherence, beauty and meaning out of the apparently random and mechanical movements of insensate atomic particles. A poetic triumph, but not (at first glance) calculated to inspire a change of heart in the reader. The poet claims to be against religion and to despise those who pray to the gods for help – and yet he subverts his own mission when he prays for help to Venus in the prelude (1.24). He ends his poem with a ghastly picture of the plague at Athens in 430 – an ending hardly likely to inspire positive joy and pleasure in the readers and one which might more easily fill them with despair in the face of such degradation and death.

There are 'ethical' passages in the poem (and many of them are printed in this edition) which advise us on matters such as the limits of pleasure, the fear of death, the correct attitude to love and sex. These ethical passages consistute a tiny proportion of a long poem, however, and one might complain that Lucretius leaves the reader adrift in a scientific sea for huge stretches of verse with little to anchor this knowledge to the 'moral' purpose of the work – were it not for the enormous force and vehemence of the ethical opinions expressed in these passages, which are often at key points of the text (beginnings and endings of books). The ethical material often persuades by mockery and rhetoric rather than abstract reasoning: the poet caricatures society types such as the bored rich man (3.1060-7), the insane lover (4.1058-191), the politician (3.995-1002), the impotent man (4. 1233-8), the brothel madam (4.1180-7), villains who murder their kinfolk for power (3.59-73) or to make the wind blow (1.80-101). This is enormously entertaining poetry – we even feel at times that the ethical material (especially the epilogue to Book 4) is drawn from the comic stage rather than Roman life; and the extremes of bad behaviour depicted do not address the more delicate issues of ethical practice which the real convert would certainly need to discuss, such as the issue of whether to engage in politics or not. Lucretius has not given us a complete 'guide to life' and yet his claim (1.936-50) that the poetry is merely the sugar on the pill of his philosophy, and that therefore his missionary purpose is paramount, is not compromised by this in any sense, and it is vital to appreciate that the whole text is of ethical as well as scientific importance.

The disproportionate amount of 'science' in the poem as against the 'ethical' sections is neatly accounted for if we remember that for Lucretius pleasure is the highest good, and that the study of nature (what the Greeks called *physiologia*) was for him a source of deep pleasure and the expression of this study in verse was also the source of his nights of serenity (1.142-5). If we were to ask Lucretius how he thought we should spend our days – which is after all the primary question in ethics – he might well say 'as I do', and urge us to devote ourselves to the study of the world. This scientific study is the source of knowledge which is the force that will remove the fear born of ignorance and the human misery which only reason can dispel: it is also a positive source of pleasure in giving us aesthetic joy in seeing the world as it is.

The choice of Epicureanism was ideal for a poet of this greatness. In the first place, it stresses the primacy of the senses and our capacity to see the truth if we will but open our eyes and look, and this approach suits well the poet with an eye for detail who will paint the world around us with clarity and sharpness of perception. We see through the poet such things as rainstorms (6.256-61), leaps of historical imagination, as in the description of early man (5.925-1447), and social behaviour such as that of the mourners (3.894-911) or the foolish lover (4.1121-91) satirised and dramatised with pitiless accuracy. In the second place, Epicureanism is primarily an ethical creed based on a scientific reading of the world; but the physics is also invested with an emotional power of its own. For the poet who found ideas interesting in their own right, who could invest cerebral concepts with both colour and emotional siginificance, this philosophy was perfect. Time after time he applies the scientific facts to the values we will infer from them, the physics to the ethics. Not content with proving our mortality, he goes on to show how we do (in fact) behave and then how we ought to behave in the face of the grim reaper; not content with explaining the facts of reproduction he tells us how to conduct our sex lives; he explains the spread of disease and then, astonishingly, ends his poem with a bleak picture of the plague at Athens. The scientific proposition that there is a finite amount of atomic variety is dramatised in the powerfully moving vignette of the cow searching for her lost calf (2.333-66). Nowhere does the poet hide behind the stark objectivity of his teaching and fail to draw the human consequences of his beliefs. The artist's eye for detail convinces the reader of the truth of what he describes and the mixture of logical argument and rhetorical diatribe hammers home the points and puts down the opposition; the indefinable emotional effects of the poetry make it the ideal medium for this instructor of minds and convertor of souls.

This selection concentrates heavily on those passages with the most obvious 'human' interest, and in the commentary I have tried to elucidate the uses of metaphor, word-play and imagery in the Latin. Lucretius claims at two points that the poetry is the honey smeared onto the bitter medicine of the philosophy. In this edition I will argue that the dichotomy does not do justice to this poet, and that in his love and admiration of the natural world there is no bitterness but a great deal of poetry, and that ultimately the question of how we ought to live is answered in the manner in which Lucretius shows us: we should live without fear of death or the gods, and in a constant state of curious joy and interest in the world around us. This *rerum natura* is freely available to all of us all of the time, and the study of it will give us understanding, the understanding will give us freedom from pain and fear, and all of this will grant us the 'divine' life of pleasure which this poem both celebrates and creates in verbal form.

SUMMARY OF THE POEM

This is a brief summary of the argument of the poem to allow readers to find their way around what is a long and complex work.

Book One

Introduction

Existence of atoms

Existence of Space

Everything is made of mattter and space

Atoms cannot be destroyed (483-634)
False theories of matter refuted

The Nature of the Universe

Book Four

Book Five

Book Six

THE METRE OF THE POEM

Latin poetry is written in a fairly rigid system of metres, all of which in turn rely on the 'quantity' of each vowel as being either long or short: a long vowel being reckoned to take twice as long to pronounce as a short vowel. A syllable is reckoned to be a single vowel sound, followed either by nothing (an 'open' syllable) or by a consonant (a 'closed' syllable): usually a single consonant following a vowel is reckoned to be the first consonant of the following syllable (e.g. *ca-li-gi-ne*) and does not affect the length of the vowel. However, where two or more consonants follow a vowel, the first one is included in the first syllable (*men-sa*) which is thus 'closed' and becomes lengthened – the exceptions being combinations of mute and liquid consonants (*b, c, g, p, t* followed by *r*; *c, p, t,* followed by *l*) which are considered as belonging to the following syllable (*pa-tris*) and need not lengthen the vowel. Diphthongs (*ae, eu, au,* etc.) are always long by nature: single vowels may be long or short by nature and may vary with inflection (e.g. the final *-a* of *mensa* is long by nature in the ablative case, short in the nominative) or they may be lengthened by position when followed by two or more consonants as indicated above (e.g. 1.100, where the short final syllable of *faustus* is lengthened by the *que* which comes immediately after it). In cases where a word ending with a vowel (or a vowel + *m* such as *iustam*) is followed by a word beginning with a vowel or *h*, the two syllables usually merge ('elide') into a single syllable (e.g. 1.51, where *ueram ad* is scanned as *uer(am) ad* (two syllables). Lucretius also allows a final 's' to be suppressed before a consonant, twice in 2.53:

> *quid dubitas quin omni' sit haec rationis potestas*

where *omnis* and *rationis* lose their final 's'. A stronger case of this is the end of 6.943 (*manantibu' stillent*) where the final 's' is suppressed and the final syllable of *manantibus* is scanned as short despite the two consonants *st-* which follow. This suppression is a concession to ordinary speech and was not adopted by later epic poets such as Virgil and Ovid.

In what follows the following signs are used:
— indicates a long syllable
∪ a short syllable
// the caesura (word-end in the middle of a foot of a hexameter).

This poem is composed in hexameters, the 'epic' metre used by Homer and all later epic poets. The line is divided into six 'feet', each of which is either a dactyl (a 'heavy' syllable followed by two 'light' syllables [—⏑⏑ in conventional notation]) or a spondee (two 'heavy' syllables [– –]). The last foot is always dissyllabic, the last syllable of all being either heavy or light. Thus a 'typical' hexameter line will run:

—⏑⏑/ —⏑⏑ / —//⏑⏑ / – – / —⏑⏑ / – –
Aéneadúm genetríx, hominúm diuúmque uolúptas

where the — sign indicates the stressed syllable at the beginning of a foot and the // sign shows the 'caesura', the word-break in the middle of a foot, usually the third.

Latin had a stress accent whereby most words were stressed on the penultimate syllable, or on the antepenultimate if the penultimate were a light syllable. Thus the first line of Book 2 of the poem would be spoken:

suáue mári mágno turbántibus aéquora uéntis

but 'scanned' metrically as:

suáue marí magnó turbántibus aéquora uéntis

Quite how the two ways of reading Latin verse blended or competed is unclear: one notes that in hexameters there is a tendency for the stress accent and the metrical ictus to collide in the first half of the line but to coincide in the second, a tendency which is however abruptly broken when the line ends with a mono-syllable as at 1.13.

SELECT BIBLIOGRAPHY

The most accessible way to read the whole Latin text of Lucretius is through the new Loeb edition (text with facing translation by M.F. Smith). I have revised the Penguin Classics translation of the whole poem (*On the Nature of the Universe*) with a new introduction, bibliography and notes. The magisterial edition of the whole poem by Cyril Bailey (Oxford, 3 vols., 1947) is still indispensable to students of this poem. Individual books have been edited as follows:

Book 1 (P.M. Brown, Bristol Classical Press, 1984).
Book 3 (E.J. Kenney, Cambridge University Press, 1971).
Book 3 (P.M. Brown, Aris and Phillips).
Book 4 (J Godwin, Aris and Phillips, 1986).
Book 5 (C.D.N. Costa, Oxford University Press, 1984).
Book 6 (J Godwin, Aris and Phillips, 1991).

The most accessible text of Epicurus (with facing translation) is to be found in the Loeb edition of Diogenes Laertius, *Lives of Eminent Philosophers*, vol.2. The best text of Epicurus is Arrighetti, *Epicuro, Opere* (2nd edition Torino, 1973) with Italian translation and notes. For the texts of the Presocratic Philosophers with translation and commentary, see Kirk, Raven and Schofield, *The Presocratic Philosophers* (Cambridge 1983). All the main texts relating to Hellenistic philosophy are to be found (with translation and discussion) in Long and Sedley, *The Hellenistic Philosophers* (2 vols, Cambridge, 1987).

The following is a list of works referred to in the commentary or consulted in the preparation of this volume and of use to the reader. The more accessible items I have marked with an asterisk.

Annas, J. and Barnes, J. *The Modes of Scepticism* (Cambridge, 1985).
Arragon, R.F., 'Poetic Art as a Philosophic Medium for Lucretius' *Essays in Criticism* 11 (1961) 371-89.
Barnes, J., *The Presocratic Philosophers* (London, 1982).
Barrett, W.S., *Euripides' Hippolytus* (Oxford, 1964).
Boyancé, P., *Lucrèce et l'epicurisme* (Paris, 1963).
Brown, P.M., *Lucretius* de rerum natura I (Bristol, 1984).
Brown, R.D., *Lucretius on Love and Sex* (Leiden, 1987).
*Carcopino, J., *Daily Life in Ancient Rome* (Harmondsworth 1986).

Classen, C.J., 'Poetry and Rhetoric in Lucretius' *Transactions of the American Philological Association* 99 (1968) 77-118.

Clay, D., *Lucretius and Epicurus* (Ithaca, 1983).

Commager, H.S. Jr., 'Lucretius' Interpretation of the Plague' *Harvard Studies in Classical Philology* LXII (1957) 105-18.

Copley, F.O., *Exclusus Amator* (American Philological Assocation Monograph 17, Baltimore 1956).

Costa, C.D.N., *Lucretius* de rerum natura *V* (Oxford, 1984).

Cox, A.S., 'Lucretius and his Message: a Study in the Prologues of the *de rerum natura*' *Greece and Rome* 18 (1971) 1-16.

Dodds, E.R., *Euripides*: Bacchae (Oxford, 1960).

*Dudley, D.R. (ed.) *Lucretius* (London, 1965).

Fitzgerald, W., 'Lucretius' cure for love in the *de rerum natura*', *Classical World* 78 (1984) 73-86.

Fowler, D.P., 'Lucretius and politics' in: Griffin and Barnes (1989) 120-50.

Fraenkel, E., *Aeschylus: Agamemnon* (Oxford, 1950).

Furley, D.J., *Two Studies in the Greek Atomists* (Princeton, 1967).

———'Nothing to us? in: Schofield, M and Striker, G. (eds) *The Norms of Nature: Studies in Hellenistic Ethics* (Cambridge, 1986) 75-91.

Gale, M.R., *Myth and Poetry in Lucretius* (Cambridge, 1994) .

Gill, C., 'The Death of Socrates' *Classical Quarterly* 23 (1973) 25-8.

Godwin, J., *Lucretius IV* (Warminster, 1986).

———Lucretius VI (Warminster 1991).

*———Lucretius On the Nature of the Universe (revision of Latham translation, Harmondsworth, 1994) .

Godwin, J., *Catullus 61-68* (Warminster, 1995).

Gowers, E., *The Loaded Table* (Oxford, 1993).

Griffin, A., *Sikyon* (Oxford, 1982).

*Griffin, J., *Latin Poets and Roman Life* (London, 1985).

Griffin, M. and Barnes, J. (edd.) *Philosophia Togata* (Oxford, 1989).

Griffin, M., 'Philosophy, Politics and Politicians' in: Griffin and Barnes (1989) 1-37.

Housman, A.E., 'Lucretiana' in *The Classical Papers of A.E. Housman* ed. J. Diggle and F.R.D. Goodyear (Cambridge, 1972) vol. 2 (1897-1914) 432-5.

*Jones, H., *The Epicurean Tradition* (London, 1989).

Kenney, E.J., 'Doctus Lucretius' *Mnemosyne* 23 (1970), 366-92.

———'Tityos and the lover' *Proceedings of the Cambridge Philological Society* 16 (1970) 44-7.

———Lucretius de rerum natura *Book 3* (Cambridge, 1971).

Kenney, E.J., *Lucretius* (Greece and Rome New Surveys in the Classics, 1977).

Kirk, G.S., Raven, J.E., Schofield, M., *The Presocratic Philosophers* (2nd edition, Cambridge, 1983).

Long, A.A., *Hellenistic Philosophy* (London, 1986).

Lyne, R.O.A.M.'Servitium Amoris' *Classical Quarterly* 29 (1979) 117-30.

The Latin Love Poets (Oxford, 1980).

Mankin, D., *Horace:* Epodes (Cambridge, 1995).

Minyard, J.D., *Lucretius and the late Republic* (Leiden, 1985).

Müller, G., 'Die Finalia der sechs Bücher des Lukrez' in: *Lucrèce* (Fondations Hardt Entretiens 24 (1977) 197-231.

Mynors, R.A.B., *Virgil Georgics* (Oxford, 1990).

Nisbet, R.G.M., and Hubbard, M. *A Commentary on Horace* Odes *Book 1* (Oxford, 1970).

————*A Commentary on Horace* Odes *Book II* (Oxford, 1978).

Ogilvie, R.M., *The Romans and their Gods* (London, 1969).

Paoli, U.E., *Rome; its People, Life and Customs* (Aberdeen, 1963).

Parker, R., *Miasma: Pollution and Purification in Early Greek Religion* (Oxford, 1983).

Penwill, J.L., 'The Ending of Sense: Death as Closure in Lucretius Book 6' *Ramus* 25 (1996) 146-69.

*Rist, J.M., *Epicurus: an Introduction* (Cambridge, 1972).

Roberts, D.H., Dunn, F.M. and Fowler, D.P., *Classical Closure: Reading the End in Greek and Latin Literature* (Princeton, 1997).

Rusten, J.S., *Thucydides*: The Peloponnesian War Book II (Cambridge, 1989).

*Santayana *Three Philosophical Poets* (Cambridge, Mass. 1910).

Schiesaro, A, *Simulacrum et Imago: gli argomenti analogici nel de rerum natura* (Pisa, 1990).

Schrijvers, P., *Horror ac Divina Voluptas: Études sur la poètique et la poèsie de Lucrèce* (Amsterdam, 1970).

————'Die Traumtheorie des Lukrez' *Mnemosyne* 33 (1980) 128-51.

Sedley, D., *Lucretius and the Transformation of Greek Wisdom* (Cambridge, 1998).

————'Lucretius' Use and Avoidance of Greek' in J.N. Adams and R.G. Mayer (eds.) *Aspects of the Language of Latin Poetry* (= Proceedings of the British Academy 93 (1999) 227-46).

Segal,C *Lucretius on death and Anxiety: Poetry and Philosophy in* de rerum natura (New Jersey, 1990).

Shackleton-Bailey, D.R., *Cicero's Letters to Atticus* vol. 1 (Cambridge, 1965).

Sharples, R.W., *Stoics, Epicureans and Sceptics: an Introduction to Hellenistic Philosophy* (London, 1996).

Snyder, J.M., *Puns and Poetry in Lucretius' de rerum natura* (Amsterdam, 1980).

Syme, R., *The Roman Revolution* (Oxford, 1939).

Taylor, C.C.W., 'All Perceptions are True' in: Schofield, M., Burnyeat, M., and Barnes, J., *Doubt and Dogmatism* (Oxford, 1980) 105-24.

*Toohey, P., *Epic Lessons: an Introduction to Ancient Didactic Poetry* (London, 1996).

Treggiari, S., *Roman Marriage* (Oxford, 1991).

Wallach, B., *Lucretius and the Diatribe against the Fear of Death* (Leiden, 1976).

Waszink, J., 'Lucretius and Poetry' *Mededelingen der koninklijke Nederlands Akademie van Wetenschafpen* (N.S. 17 [1954] 243-57).

*West, D., *The Imagery and Poetry of Lucretius* (Edinburgh, 1969).

West, M.L., *Hesiod* Theogony (Oxford, 1966)

Williams, G., *Tradition and Originality in Roman Poetry* (Oxford, 1968).

*Wiseman, T.P., 'The two worlds of Titus Lucretius' in: *Cinna the Poet and other Roman essays* (Leicester, 1974).

Book One

Preface invoking the goddess Venus

Aeneadum genetrix, hominum diuumque uoluptas
alma Venus, caeli subter labentia signa
quae mare nauigerum, quae terras frugiferentis
concelebras, per te quoniam genus omne animantum
concipitur uisitque exortum lumina solis: 5
te, dea, te fugiunt uenti, te nubila caeli
aduentumque tuum tibi suauis daedala tellus
summittit flores, tibi rident aequora ponti
placatumque nitet diffuso lumine caelum.
nam simul ac species patefactast uerna diei   10
et reserata uiget genitabilis aura fauoni
aeriae primum uolucres te, diua, tuumque
significant initum perculsae corda tua ui.
inde ferae pecudes persultant pabula laeta
et rapidos tranant amnis: ita capta lepore   15
te sequitur cupide quo quamque inducere pergis.
denique, per maria ac montis fluuiosque rapacis
frondiferasque domos auium camposque uirentis,
omnibus incutiens blandum per pectora amorem,
efficis ut cupide generatim saecla propagent.   20
quae quoniam rerum naturam sola gubernas,
nec sine te quicquam dias in luminis oras
exoritur neque fit laetum neque amabile quicquam,
te sociam studeo scribendis uersibus esse
quos ego de rerum natura pangere conor   25
Memmiadae nostro, quem tu, dea, tempore in omni
omnibus ornatum uoluisti excellere rebus.
quo magis aeternum da dictis, diua, leporem.
effice ut interea fera moenera militiai
per maria ac terras omnis sopita quiescant;   30
nam tu sola potes tranquilla pace iuuare
mortalis, quoniam belli fera moenera Mauors
armipotens regit, in gremium qui saepe tuum se

reiicit aeterno deuinctus uulnere amoris
atque ita suspiciens tereti ceruice reposta   35
pascit amore auidos inhians in te, dea, uisus,
eque tuo pendet resupini spiritus ore.
hunc tu, diua, tuo recubantem corpore sancto
circumfusa super, suauis ex ore loquellas
funde petens placidam Romanis, incluta, pacem: 40
nam neque nos agere hoc patriai tempore iniquo
possumus aequo animo nec Memmi clara propago
talibus in rebus communi desse saluti.
omnis enim per se diuom natura necessest
immortali aeuo summa cum pace fruatur   45
semota ab nostris rebus seiunctaque longe;
nam priuata dolore omni, priuata periclis,
ipsa suis pollens opibus, nil indiga nostri,
nec bene promeritis capitur neque tangitur ira.

Address to the reader

quod superest, uacuas auris animumque sagacem   50
semotum a curis adhibe ueram ad rationem,
ne mea dona tibi studio disposta fideli
intellecta prius quam sint contempta relinquas.
nam tibi de summa caeli ratione deumque
disserere incipiam, et rerum primordia pandam,   55
unde omnis natura creet res auctet alatque
quoue eadem rursum natura perempta resoluat,
quae nos materiem et genitalia corpora rebus
reddunda in ratione uocare et semina rerum
appellare suemus et haec eadem usurpare   60
corpora prima, quod ex illis sunt omnia primis.

The achievement of Epicurus

humana ante oculos foede cum uita iaceret
in terris oppressa graui sub religione,
quae caput a caeli regionibus ostendebat
horribili super aspectu mortalibus instans,   65
primum Graius homo mortalis tollere contra
est oculos ausus primusque obsistere contra,
quem neque fama deum nec fulmine nec minitanti
murmure compressit caelum, sed eo magis acrem

inritat animi uirtutem, effringere ut arta   70
naturae primus portarum claustra cupiret.
ergo uiuida uis animi peruicit, et extra
processit longe flammantia moenia mundi
atque omne immensum peragrauit mente animoque,
unde refert nobis uictor quid possit oriri,   75
quid nequeat, finita potestas denique cuique
quanam sit ratione atque alte terminus haerens.
quare religio pedibus subiecta uicissim
obteritur, nos exaequat uictoria caelo.

The evils of religion – the sacrifice of Iphigeneia

illud in his rebus uereor, ne forte rearis   80
impia te rationis inire elementa uiamque
indugredi sceleris. quod contra saepius illa
religio peperit scelerosa atque impia facta:
Aulide quo pacto Triuiai uirginis aram
Iphianassai turparunt sanguine foede   85
ductores Danaum delecti, prima uirorum.
cui simul infula uirgineos circumdata comptus
ex utraque pari malarum parte profusast,
et maestum simul ante aras adstare parentem
sensit et hunc propter ferrum celare ministros   90
aspectuque suo lacrimas effundere civis,
muta metu terram genibus summissa petebat.
nec miserae prodesse in tali tempore quibat
quod patrio princeps donarat nomine regem;
nam sublata uirum manibus tremibundaque ad aras   95
deductast, non ut sollemni more sacrorum
perfecto posset claro comitari hymenaeo,
sed casta inceste nubendi tempore in ipso
hostia concideret mactatu maesta parentis –
exitus ut classi felix faustusque daretur.   100
tantum religio potuit suadere malorum.

The poet's purpose

nunc age quod superest cognosce atque clarius audi.
nec me animi fallit quam sit obscura; sed acri
percussit thyrso laudis spes magna meum cor,
et simul incussit suavem mi in pectus amorem

3

Musarum, quo nunc instinctus mente vigenti 925
avia Pieridum peragro loca nullius ante
trita solo. iuvat integros accedere fontis
atque haurire, iuvatque novos decerpere flores
insignemque meo capiti petere inde coronam
unde prius nulli velarint tempora Musae: 930
primum quod magnis doceo de rebus et artis
religionum animum nodis exsolvere pergo,
deinde quod obscura de re tam lucida pango
carmina musaeo contingens cuncta lepore.
id quoque enim non ab nulla ratione videtur; 935
nam veluti pueris absinthia taetra medentes
cum dare conantur, prius oras pocula circum
contingunt mellis dulci flavoque liquore,
ut puerorum aetas inprovida ludificetur
labrorum tenus, interea perpotet amarum 940
absinthi laticem deceptaque non capiatur,
sed potius tali tactu recreata valescat,
sic ego nunc, quoniam haec ratio plerumque videtur
tristior esse quibus non est tractata, retroque
volgus abhorret ab hac, volui tibi suaviloquenti 945
carmine Pierio rationem exponere nostram
et quasi musaeo dulci contingere melle
si tibi forte animum tali ratione tenere
versibus in nostris possem, dum percipis omnem
naturam rerum qua constet compta figura. 950

Book Two

The Good Life

suaue, mari magno turbantibus aequora uentis,
e terra magnum alterius spectare laborem;
non quia uexari quemquamst iucunda uoluptas,
sed quibus ipsa malis careas quia cernere suaue est.
suaue etiam belli certamina magna tueri 5
per campos instructa tua sine parte pericli.
sed nil dulcius est bene quam munita tenere

edita doctrina sapientum templa serena,
despicere unde queas alios passimque uidere
errare atque uiam palantis quaerere uitae,   10
certare ingenio, contendere nobilitate,
noctes atque dies niti praestante labore
ad summas emergere opes rerumque potiri.
o miseras hominum mentes! o pectora caeca!
qualibus in tenebris uitae quantisque periclis   15
degitur hoc aeui quodcumque est! nonne uidere
nil aliud sibi naturam latrare, nisi utqui
corpore seiunctus dolor absit, mensque fruatur
iucundo sensu cura semota metuque?
ergo corpoream ad naturam pauca uidemus   20
esse opus omnino, quae demant cumque dolorem,
delicias quoque uti multas substernere possint;
gratius interdum neque natura ipsa requirit,
si non aurea sunt iuuenum simulacra per aedes
lampadas igniferas manibus retinentia dextris,   25
lumina nocturnis epulis ut suppeditentur,
nec domus argento fulget auroque renidet
nec citharae reboant laqueata aurataque templa,
cum tamen inter se prostrati in gramine molli
propter aquae riuum sub ramis arboris altae   30
non magnis opibus iucunde corpora curant,
praesertim cum tempestas adridet et anni
tempora conspergunt uiridantis floribus herbas.
nec calidae citius decedunt corpore febres,
textilibus si in picturis ostroque rubenti   35
iacteris, quam si in plebeia ueste cubandum est.
quapropter quoniam nil nostro in corpore gazae
proficiunt neque nobilitas nec gloria regni,
quod superest, animo quoque nil prodesse putandum:
si non forte, tuas legiones per loca campi   40
feruere cum uideas belli simulacra cientis,
subsidiis magnis et equum ui constabilitas,
ornatas armis pariter pariterque animatas,
his tibi tum rebus timefactae religiones
effugiunt animo pauidae, mortisque timores   45
tum uacuum pectus linquunt curaque solutum.
quod si ridicula haec ludibriaque esse uidemus

re ueraque metus hominum curaeque sequaces
nec metuunt sonitus armorum nec fera tela
audacterque inter reges rerumque potentis   50
uersantur neque fulgorem reuerentur ab auro
nec clarum uestis splendorem purpureai,
quid dubitas quin omni' sit haec rationi' potestas,
omnis cum in tenebris praesertim uita laboret?
nam ueluti pueri trepidant atque omnia caecis   55
in tenebris metuunt, sic nos in luce timemus
interdum nilo quae sunt metuenda magis quam
quae pueri in tenebris pauitant finguntque futura.
hunc igitur terrorem animi tenebrasque necessest
non radii solis neque lucida tela diei   60
discutiant, sed naturae species ratioque.

Atomic variety: the lost calf

nunc age iam deinceps cunctarum exordia rerum
qualia sint et quam longe distantia formis
percipe, multigenis quam sint uariata figuris;   335
non quo multa parum simili sint praedita forma,
sed quia non uolgo paria omnibus omnia constant.
nec mirum; nam cum sit eorum copia tanta
ut neque finis, uti docui, neque summa sit ulla,
debent nimirum non omnibus omnia prorsum   340
esse pari filo similique adfecta figura.
praeterea genus humanum mutaeque natantes
squamigerum pecudes et laeta armenta feraeque
et uariae uolucres, laetantia quae loca aquarum
concelebrant circum ripas fontisque lacusque,   345
et quae peruolgant nemora auia peruolitantes –
quorum unum quiduis generatim sumere perge:
inuenies tamen inter se differre figuris.
nec ratione alia proles cognoscere matrem
nec mater posset prolem: quod posse uidemus   350
nec minus atque homines inter se nota cluere.
nam saepe ante deum uitulus delubra decora
turicremas propter mactatus concidit aras,
sanguinis expirans calidum de pectore flumen;
at mater uiridis saltus orbata peragrans   355
quaerit humi pedibus uestigia pressa bisulcis,

6

omnia conuisens oculis loca si queat usquam
conspicere amissum fetum, completque querellis
frondiferum nemus adsistens et crebra revisit
ad stabulum desiderio perfixa iuvenci;   360
nec tenerae salices atque herbae rore uigentes
fluminaque illa queunt summis labentia ripis
oblectare animum subitamque auertere curam,
nec uitulorum aliae species per pabula laeta
deriuare queunt animum curaque leuare: 365
usque adeo quiddam proprium notumque requirit.
praeterea teneri tremulis cum uocibus haedi
cornigeras norunt matres agnique petulci
balantum pecudes: ita quod natura reposcit,
ad sua quisque fere decurrunt ubera lactis.   370

Book Three

Death is nothing to us

nil igitur mors est ad nos neque pertinet hilum,   830
quandoquidem natura animi mortalis habetur;
et, uelut anteacto nil tempore sensimus aegri,
ad confligendum uenientibus undique Poenis,
omnia cum belli trepido concussa tumultu
horrida contremuere sub altis aetheris auris,   835
in dubioque fuere utrorum ad regna cadendum
omnibus humanis esset terraque marique,
sic, ubi non erimus, cum corporis atque animai
discidium fuerit, quibus e sumus uniter apti,
scilicet haud nobis quicquam, qui non erimus tum,   840
accidere omnino poterit sensumque mouere,
non si terra mari miscebitur et mare caelo.
et si iam nostro sentit de corpore postquam
distractast animi natura animaeque potestas,
nil tamen est ad nos, qui comptu coniugioque   845
corporis atque animae consistimus uniter apti.
nec, si materiem nostram collegerit aetas
post obitum rursumque ut sita nunc est,

7

atque iterum nobis fuerint data lumina uitae,
pertineat quicquam tamen ad nos id quoque factum   850
interrupta semel ¢um sit repetentia nostri.
et nunc nil ad nos de nobis attinet, ante
qui fuimus, neque iam de illis nos adficit angor.
nam cum respicias immensi temporis omne
praeteritum spatium, tum motus materiai   855
multimodi quam sint, facile hoc adcredere possis,
semina saepe in eodem, ut nunc sunt, ordine posta
haec eadem, quibus e nunc nos sumus, ante fuisse.
nec memori tamen id quimus reprehendere mente;
inter enim iectast uitai pausa, uageque   860
deerrarunt passim motus ab sensibus omnes.
debet enim, misere si forte aegreque futurumst,
ipse quoque esse in eo tum tempore, cui male possit
accidere. id quoniam mors eximit, esseque probet
illum cui possint incommoda conciliari,   865
scire licet nobis nil esse in morte timendum,
nec miserum fieri qui non est posse, neque hilum
differre an nullo fuerit iam tempore natus,
mortalem uitam mors cum immortalis ademit.

It does not matter what becomes of our corpse

proinde ubi se uideas hominem indignarier ipsum   870
post mortem fore ut aut putescat corpore posto
aut flammis interfiat malisve ferarum,
scire licet non sincerum sonere atque subesse
caecum aliquem cordi stimulum, quamuis neget ipse
credere se quemquam sibi sensum in morte futurum;   875
non, ut opinor, enim dat quod promittit et unde,
non radicitus e uita se tollit et eicit,
sed facit esse sui quiddam super inscius ipse.
uiuus enim sibi cum proponit quisque futurum,
corpus uti uolucres lacerent in morte feraeque,   880
ipse sui miseret; neque enim se diuidit illim
nec remouet satis a proiecto corpore, et illum
se fingit sensuque suo contaminat astans.
hinc indignatur se mortalem esse creatum,
nec uidet in uera nullum fore morte alium se   885
qui possit uiuus sibi se lugere peremptum

8

stansque iacentem se lacerari uriue dolere.
nam si in morte malumst malis morsuque ferarum
tractari, non inuenio qui non sit acerbum
ignibus impositum calidis torrescere flammis   890
aut in melle situm suffocari atque rigere
frigore, cum summo gelidi cubat aequore saxi,
urgeriue superne obtritum pondere terrae.

The lament of the mourners

'iam iam non domus accipiet te laeta, neque uxor
optima, nec dulces occurrent oscula nati   895
praeripere et tacita pectus dulcedine tangent.
non poteris factis florentibus esse, tuisque
praesidium. misero misere' aiunt 'omnia ademit
una dies infesta tibi tot praemia uitae.'
illud in his rebus non addunt: 'nec tibi earum   900
iam desiderium rerum super insidet una.'
quod bene si uideant animo dictisque sequantur,
dissoluant animi magno se angore metuque.
'tu quidem, ut es leto sopitus, sic eris aeui
quod superest cunctis priuatu' doloribus aegris;   905
at nos horrifico cinefactum te prope busto
insatiabiliter defleuimus, aeternumque
nulla dies nobis maerorem e pectore demet.'
illud ab hoc igitur quaerendum est quid sit amari
tanto opere, ad somnum si res redit atque quietem   910
cur quisqam aeterno possit tabescere luctu.
hoc etiam faciunt ubi discubuere tenentque
pocula saepe homines et inumbrant ora coronis,
ex animo ut dicant: 'breuis hic est fructus homullis;
iam fuerit neque post umquam reuocare licebit.'   915
tamquam in morte mali cum primis hoc sit eorum,
quod sitis exurat miseros atque arida torrat,
aut aliae cuius desiderium insideat rei.
nec sibi enim quisquam tum se uitamque requirit,
cum pariter mens et corpus sopita quiescunt: 920
nam licet aeternum per nos sic esse soporem,
nec desiderium nostri nos adficit ullum,
et tamen haudquaquam nostros tunc illa per artus
longe ab sensiferis primordia motibus errant,

cum correptus homo ex somno se colligit ipse.   925
multo igitur mortem minus ad nos esse putandumst,
si minus esse potest quam quod nil esse uidemus;
maior enim turba et disiectus materiai
consequitur leto, nec quisquam expergitus exstat,
frigida quem semel est uitai pausa secuta.   930

Nature answers those reluctant to die

denique si uocem rerum natura repente
mittat et hoc alicui nostrum sic increpet ipsa
'quid tibi tanto operest, mortalis, quod nimis aegris
luctibus indulges? quid mortem congemis ac fles?
nam si grata fuit tibi uita anteacta priorque   935
et non omnia pertusum congesta quasi in uas
commoda perfluxere atque ingrata interiere,
cur non ut plenus uitae conuiua recedis
aequo animoque capis securam, stulte, quietem?
sin ea quae fructus cumque es periere profusa   940
uitaque in offensast, cur amplius addere quaeris
rursum quod pereat male et ingratum occidat omne,
non potius uitae finem facis atque laboris?
nam tibi praeterea quod machiner inueniamque
quod placeat, nil est: eadem sunt omnia semper.   945
si tibi non annis corpus iam marcet et artus
confecti languent, eadem tamen omnia restant,
omnia si perges uiuendo uincere saecla,
atque etiam potius, si numquam sis moriturus';
quid respondemus, nisi iustam intendere litem   950
naturam et ueram uerbis exponere causam?
grandior hic uero si iam seniorque queratur
atque obitum lamentetur miser amplius aequo,
non merito inclamet magis et uoce increpet acri?
'aufer abhinc lacrimas, baratre, et compesce querellas!   955
omnia perfunctus uitai praemia marces;
sed quia semper aues quod abest, praesentia temnis,
inperfecta tibi elapsast ingrataque uita,
et nec opinanti mors ad caput adstitit ante
quam satur ac plenus possis discedere rerum.   960
nunc aliena tua tamen aetate omnia mitte
aequo animoque agedum iam annis concede: necessest.'

10

iure, ut opinor, agat, iure increpet inciletque;
cedit enim rerum nouitate extrusa vetustas
semper, et ex aliis aliud reparare necessest; 965
nec quisquam in barathrum nec Tartara deditur atra:
materies opus est ut crescant postera saecla,
quae tamen omnia te uita perfuncta sequentur;
nec minus ergo ante haec quam tu cecidere, cadentque.
sic alid ex alio numquam desistet oriri 970
uitaque mancipio nulli datur, omnibus usu.
respice item quam nil ad nos anteacta uetustas
temporis aeterni fuerit, quam nascimur ante.
hoc igitur speculum nobis natura futuri
temporis exponit post mortem denique nostram. 975
numquid ibi horribile apparet? num triste uidetur
quicquam? non omni somno securius exstat?

The fables of punishment after death

atque ea nimirum quaecumque Acherunte profundo
prodita sunt esse, in uita sunt omnia nobis.
nec miser impendens magnum timet aere saxum 980
Tantalus, ut famast, cassa formidine torpens;
sed magis in uita diuom metus urget inanis
mortalis, casumque timent quem cuique ferat fors.
nec Tityon uolucres ineunt Acherunte iacentem
nec quod sub magno scrutentur pectore quicquam 985
perpetuam aetatem possunt reperire profecto.
quamlibet immani proiectu corporis exstet,
qui non sola nouem dispessis iugera membris
obtineat, sed qui terrai totius orbem
non tamen aeternum poterit perferre dolorem 990
nec praebere cibum proprio de corpore semper.
sed Tityos nobis hic est, in amore iacentem
quem uolucres lacerant atque exest anxius angor
aut alia quauis scindunt cuppedine curae.
Sisyphus in uita quoque nobis ante oculos est, 995
qui petere a populo fasces saevasque secures
imbibit et semper uictus tristisque recedit.
nam petere imperium quod inanest nec datur umquam
atque in eo semper durum sufferre laborem,
hoc est adverso nixantem trudere monte 1000

saxum quod tamen e summo iam uertice rursum
uoluitur et plani raptim petit aequora campi.
deinde animi ingratam naturam pascere semper
atque explere bonis rebus satiareque numquam –
quod faciunt nobis annorum tempora, circum   1005
cum redeunt fetusque ferunt uariosque lepores,
nec tamen explemur uitai fructibus umquam –
hoc, ut opinor, id est, aeuo florente puellas
quod memorant laticem pertusum congerere in uas,
quod tamen expleri nulla ratione potestur.   1010
Cerberus et Furiae iam uero et lucis egestas,
Tartarus horriferos eructans faucibus aestus –
qui neque sunt usquam nec possunt esse profecto.
sed metus in uita poenarum pro male factis
est insignibus insignis, scelerisque luella –   1015
carcer et horribilis de saxo iactu' deorsum,
uerbera carnifices robur pix lammina taedae;
quae tamen etsi absunt, at mens sibi conscia factis
praemetuens adhibet stimulos torretque flagellis,
nec uidet interea qui terminus esse malorum   1020
possit nec quae sit poenarum denique finis,
atque eadem metuit magis haec ne in morte grauescant.
hic Acherusia fit stultorum denique uita.

Book Four

Dreaming

et quo quisque fere studio deuinctus adhaeret,
aut quibus in rebus multum sumus ante morati,
atque in ea ratione fuit contenta magis mens,
in somnis eadem plerumque uidemur obire: 965
causidici causas agere et componere leges,
induperatores pugnare ac proelia obire,
nautae contractum cum uentis degere duellum,
nos agere hoc autem et naturam quaerere rerum
semper et inuentam patriis exponere chartis.   970
cetera sic studia atque artes plerumque uidentur

in somnis animos hominum frustrata tenere.
et quicumque dies multos ex ordine ludis
adsiduas dederunt operas, plerumque uidemus,
cum iam destiterunt ea sensibus usurpare,   975
relicuas tamen esse uias in mente patentis,
qua possint eadem rerum simulacra uenire.
per multos itaque illa dies eadem obuersantur
ante oculos, etiam uigilantes ut uideantur
cernere saltantis et mollis membra mouentis,   980
et citharae liquidum carmen chordasque loquentis
auribus accipere, et consessum cernere eundem
scenaique simul uarios splendere decores.

Romantic love

haec Venus est nobis; hinc autemst nomen amoris;
hinc illaec primum Veneris dulcedinis in cor
stillavit gutta, et successit frigida cura.   1060
nam si abest quod ames, praesto simulacra tamen sunt
illius, et nomen dulce obuersatur ad auris.
sed fugitare decet simulacra et pabula amoris
absterrere sibi atque alio conuertere mentem
et iacere umorem conlectum in corpora quaeque,   1065
nec retinere, semel conuersum unius amore,
et seruare sibi curam certumque dolorem;
ulcus enim uiuescit et inueterascit alendo,
inque dies gliscit furor atque aerumna gravescit,
si non prima nouis conturbes uolnera plagis   1070
uolgiuagaque uagus Venere ante recentia cures
aut alio possis animi traducere motus.
nec Veneris fructu caret is qui uitat amorem,
sed potius quae sunt sine poena commoda sumit;
nam certe purast sanis magis inde uoluptas   1075
quam miseris. etenim potiundi tempore in ipso
fluctuat incertis erroribus ardor amantum,
nec constat quid primum oculis manibusque fruantur.
quod petiere, premunt arte faciuntque dolorem
corporis, et dentes inlidunt saepe labellis   1080
osculaque adfligunt, quia non est pura uoluptas
et stimuli subsunt qui instigant laedere id ipsum,
quodcumque est, rabies unde illaec germina surgunt.

sed leviter poenas frangit Venus inter amorem,
blandaque refrenat morsus admixta uoluptas;   1085
namque in eo spes est, unde est ardoris origo,
restingui quoque posse ab eodem corpore flammam.
quod fieri contra totum natura repugnat:
unaque res haec est, cuius quam plurima habemus,
tam magis ardescit dira cuppedine pectus.   1090
nam cibus atque umor membris adsumitur intus;
quae quoniam certas possunt obsidere partis,
hoc facile expletur laticum frugumque cupido.
ex hominis uero facie pulchroque colore
nil datur in corpus praeter simulacra fruendum   1095
tenuia; quae uento spes raptast saepe misella.
ut bibere in somnis sitiens quom quaerit, et umor
non datur, ardorem qui membris stinguere possit,
sed laticum simulacra petit frustraque laborat
in medioque sitit torrenti flumine potans,   1100
sic in amore Venus simulacris ludit amantis,
nec satiare queunt spectando corpora curam
nec manibus quicquam teneris abradere membris
possunt errantes incerti corpore toto.
denique cum membris conlatis flore fruuntur   1105
aetatis, iam cum praesagit gaudia corpus
atque in eost Venus ut muliebria conserat arua,
adfigunt auide corpus iunguntque saliuas
oris et inspirant pressantes dentibus ora –
nequiquam, quoniam nil inde abradere possunt   1110
nec penetrare et abire in corpus corpore toto;
nam facere interdum uelle et certare uidentur:
usque adeo cupide in Veneris compagibus haerent,
membra uoluptatis dum ui labefacta liquescunt.
tandem ubi se erupit neruis conlecta cupido,   1115
parua fit ardoris uiolenti pausa parumper.
inde redit rabies eadem et furor ille reuisit,
cum sibi quod cupiant ipsi contingere quaerunt,
nec reperire malum id possunt quae machina uincat:
usque adeo incerti tabescunt uolnere caeco.   1120
adde quod absumunt uiris pereuntque labore,
adde quod alterius sub nutu degitur aetas.
labitur interea res et Babylonica fiunt,

languent officia atque aegrotat fama vacillans.
unguenta et pulchra in pedibus Sicyonia rident; 1125
scilicet et grandes uiridi cum luce zmaragdi
auro includuntur, teriturque thalassina uestis
adsidue et Veneris sudorem exercita potat;
et bene parta patrum fiunt anademata, mitrae,
interdum in pallam ac Melitensia Coaque vertunt; 1130
eximia ueste et uictu conuiuia, ludi,
pocula crebra, unguenta, coronae, serta parantur –
nequiquam, quoniam medio de fonte leporum
surgit amari aliquid quod in ipsis floribus angat,
aut cum conscius ipse animus se forte remordet 1135
desidiose agere aetatem lustrisque perire,
aut quod in ambiguo uerbum iaculata reliquit
quod cupido adfixum cordi uiuescit ut ignis,
aut nimium iactare oculos aliumve tueri
quod putat, in uoltuque uidet uestigia risus. 1140
atque in amore mala haec proprio summeque secundo
inueniuntur; in aduerso uero atque inopi sunt,
prendere quae possis oculorum lumine operto,
innumerabilia; ut melius uigilare sit ante,
qua docui ratione, cauereque ne inliciaris. 1145
nam uitare, plagas in amoris ne laciamur,
non ita difficile est quam captum retibus ipsos
exire et ualidos Veneris perrumpere nodos.
et tamen implicitus quoque possis inque peditus
effugere infestum, nisi tute tibi obuius obstes 1150
et praetermittas animi uitia omnia primum
aut quae corpori' sunt eius, quam praepetis ac uis.
nam faciunt homines plerumque cupidine caeci
et tribuunt ea quae non sunt his commoda uere.
multimodis igitur prauas turpisque uidemus 1155
esse in deliciis summoque in honore uigere.
atque alios alii inrident Veneremque suadent
ut placent, quoniam foedo adflictentur amore,
nec sua respiciunt miseri mala maxima saepe.
nigra 'melichrus' est, inmunda et fetida 'acosmos', 1160
caesia 'Palladium', neruosa et lignea 'dorcas'
paruula pumilio 'chariton mia' 'tota merum sal',
magna atque immanis 'cataplexis plenaque honoris'.

balba loqui non quit – 'traulizi'; muta 'pudens' est.
at flagrans odiosa loquacula 'Lampadium' fit;   1165
'ischnon eromenion' tum fit cum uiuere non quit
prae macie; 'rhadine' uerost iam mortua tussi;
at tumida et mammosa 'Ceres' est 'ipsa ab Iaccho',
simula 'Silena ac saturast', labeosa 'philema'.
cetera de genere hoc longum si dicere coner.   1170
sed tamen esto iam quantouis oris honore,
cui Veneris membris uis omnibus exoriatur:
nempe aliae quoque sunt; nempe hac sine uiximus ante;
nempe eadem facit – et scimus facere – omnia turpi,
et miseram taetris se suffit odoribus ipsa,   1175
quam famulae longe fugitant furtimque cachinnant..
at lacrimans exclusus amator limina saepe
floribus et sertis operit postisque superbos
unguit amaracino et foribus miser oscula figit;
quem si, iam ammissum, uenientem offenderit aura   1180
una modo, causas abeundi quaerat honestas
et meditat diu cadat alte sumpta querella,
stultitiaque ibi se damnet, tribuisse quod illi
plus uideat quam mortali concedere par est.
nec Veneres nostras hoc fallit: quo magis ipsae   1185
omnia summo opere hos uitae postscaenia celant
quos retinere uolunt adstrictosque esse in amore –
nequiquam, quoniam tu animo tamen omnia possis
protrahere in lucem atque omnis inquirere risus,
et, si bello animost et non odiosa, uicissim   1190
praetermittere et humanis concedere rebus.

Book Five

The achievements of Epicurus

quis potis est dignum pollenti pectore carmen
condere pro rerum maiestate hisque repertis?
quisue ualet uerbis tantum qui fingere laudes
pro meritis eius possit qui talia nobis
pectore parta suo quaesitaque praemia liquit?   5

nemo, ut opinor, erit mortali corpore cretus.
nam si, ut ipsa petit maiestas cognita rerum,
dicendum est, deus ille fuit, deus, inclute Memmi,
qui princeps uitae rationem inuenit eam quae
nunc appellatur sapientia, quique per artem   10
fluctibus e tantis uitam tantisque tenebris
in tam tranquillo et tam clara luce locauit.
confer enim diuina aliorum antique reperta.
namque Ceres fertur fruges Liberque liquoris
uitigeni laticem mortalibus instituisse;   15
cum tamen his posset sine rebus uita manere,
ut fama est aliquas etiam nunc uiuere gentis.
at bene non poterat sine puro pectore uiui;
quo magis hic merito nobis deus esse uidetur,
ex quo nunc etiam per magnas didita gentis   20
dulcia permulcent animos solacia uitae.
Herculis antistare autem si facta putabis,
longius a uera multo ratione ferere.
quid Nemeaeus enim nobis nunc magnus hiatus
ille leonis obesset et horrens Arcadius sus?   25
denique quid Cretae taurus Lernaeaque pestis
hydra uenenatis posset uallata colubris?
quidve tripectora tergemini uis Geryonai

* * * * *

tanto opere officerent nobis Stymphala colentes,
et Diomedis equi spirantes naribus ignem   30
Thracis Bistoniasque plagas atque Ismara propter?
aureaque Hesperidum seruans fulgentia mala
asper, acerba tuens, immani corpore serpens
arboris amplexus stirpem, quid denique obesset
propter Atlanteum litus pelagique seuera,   35
quo neque noster adit quisquam nec barbarus audet?
cetera de genere hoc quae sunt portenta perempta,
si non uicta forent, quid tandem uiua nocerent?
nil, ut opinor: ita ad satiatem terra ferarum
nunc etiam scatit et trepido terrore repleta est   40
per nemora ac montes magnos siluasque profundas;
quae loca uitandi plerumque est nostra potestas.
at nisi purgatumst pectus, quae proelia nobis

atque pericula tunc ingratis insinuandum!
quantae tum scindunt hominem cuppedinis acres   45
sollicitum curae quantique perinde timores!
quidue superbia spurcitia ac petulantia? quantas
efficiunt clades! quid luxus desidiaeque?
haec igitur qui cuncta subegerit ex animoque
expulerit dictis, non armis, nonne decebit   50
hunc hominem numero diuom dignarier esse?
cum bene praesertim multa ac diuinitus ipsis
immortalibu' de diuis dare dicta suerit
atque omnem rerum naturam pandere dictis.

The world is too full of flaws to be divinely created

quod si iam rerum ignorem primordia quae sint   195
hoc tamen ex ipsis caeli rationibus ausim
confirmare aliisque ex rebus reddere multis,
nequaquam nobis diuinitus esse paratam
naturam rerum: tanta stat praedita culpa.
principio quantum caeli tegit impetus ingens,   200
inde auidam partem montes siluaeque ferarum
possedere, tenent rupes uastaeque paludes
et mare quod late terrarum distinet oras.
inde duas porro prope partis fervidus ardor
adsiduusque geli casus mortalibus aufert.   205
quod superest arui, tamen id natura sua ui
sentibus obducat, ni uis humana resistat,
uitai causa ualido consueta bidenti
ingemere et terram pressis proscindere aratris.
si non fecundas uertentes uomere glebas   210
terraique solum subigentes cimus ad ortus,
sponte sua nequeant liquidas existere in auras;
et tamen interdum magno quaesita labore
cum iam per terras frondent atque omnia florent,
aut nimiis torret feruoribus aetherius sol   215
aut subiti peremunt imbres gelidaeque pruinae,
flabraque uentorum uiolento turbine uexant.
praeterea genus horriferum natura ferarum
humanae genti infestum terraque marique
cur alit atque auget? cur anni tempora morbos   220
adportant? quare mors inmatura uagatur?

tum porro puer, ut saeuis proiectus ab undis
nauita, nudus, humi iacet, infans, indigus omni
uitali auxilio, cum primum in luminis oras
nixibus ex aluo matris natura profudit,   225
uagituque locum lugubri complet, ut aequumst
cui tantum in uita restet transire malorum.
at uariae crescunt pecudes armenta feraeque,
nec crepitacillis opus est, nec cuiquam adhibendast
almae nutricis blanda atque infracta loquella,   230
nec uarias quaerunt uestes pro tempore caeli,
denique non armis opus est, non moenibus altis,
qui sua tutentur, quando omnibus omnia large
tellus ipsa parit naturaque daedala rerum.

Book Six

The Plague at Athens

Haec ratio quondam morborum et mortifer aestus
finibus in Cecropis funestos reddidit agros
uastauitque uias, exhausit ciuibus urbem.   1140
nam penitus ueniens Aegypti finibus ortus,
aëra permensus multum camposque natantis,
incubuit tandem populo Pandionis omni.
inde cateruatim morbo mortique dabantur.
principio caput incensum feruore gerebant   1145
et duplicis oculos suffusa luce rubentes.
sudabant etiam fauces intrinsecus atrae
sanguine et ulceribus uocis uia saepta coibat
atque animi interpres manabat lingua cruore
debilitata malis, motu grauis, aspera tactu.   1150
inde ubi per fauces pectus complerat et ipsum
morbida uis in cor maestum confluxerat aegris,
omnia tum uero uitai claustra lababant.
spiritus ore foras taetrum uoluebat odorem,
rancida quo perolent proiecta cadauera ritu.   1155
atque animi prorsum tum uires totius, omne
languebat corpus leti iam limine in ipso.

intolerabilibusque malis erat anxius angor
adsidue comes et gemitu commixta querella,
singultusque frequens noctem per saepe diemque   1160
corripere adsidue neruos et membra coactans
dissoluebat eos, defessos ante, fatigans.
nec nimio cuiquam posses ardore tueri
corporis in summo summam feruescere partem,
sed potius tepidum manibus proponere tactum   1165
et simul ulceribus quasi inustis omne rubere
corpus, ut est per membra sacer dum diditur ignis.
intima pars hominum uero flagrabat ad ossa,
flagrabat stomacho flamma ut fornacibus intus.
nil adeo posses cuiquam leue tenueque membris   1170
uertere in utilitatem, at uentum et frigora semper.
in fluuios partim gelidos ardentia morbo
membra dabant nudum iacientes corpus in undas.
multi praecipites lymphis putealibus alte
inciderunt ipso uenientes ore patente: 1175
insedabiliter sitis arida corpora mersans
aequabat multum paruis umoribus imbrem.
nec requies erat ulla mali: defessa iacebant
corpora. mussabat tacito medicina timore,
quippe patentia cum totiens ardentia morbis   1180
lumina uersarent oculorum expertia somno.
multaque praeterea mortis tum signa dabantur:
perturbata animi mens in maerore metuque,
triste supercilium, furiosus uoltus et acer,
sollicitae porro plenaeque sonoribus aures,   1185
creber spiritus aut ingens raroque coortus,
sudorisque madens per collum splendidus umor,
tenvia sputa minuta, croci contacta colore
salsaque per fauces rauca uix edita tussi.
in manibus vero nervi trahere et tremere artus   1190
a pedibusque minutatim succedere frigus
non dubitabat. item ad supremum denique tempus
conpressae nares, nasi primoris acumen
tenue, cauati oculi, caua tempora, frigida pellis
duraque in archiatri tactum: frons tenta tumebat.   1195
nec nimio rigida post artus morte iacebant.
octauoque fere candenti lumine solis

aut etiam nona reddebant lampade uitam.
quorum siquis, ut est, uitarat funera leti,
ulceribus taetris et nigra proluuie alui   1200
posterius tamen hunc tabes letumque manebat,
aut etiam multus capitis cum saepe dolore
corruptus sanguis expletis naribus ibat.
huc hominis totae uires corpusque fluebat.
profluvium porro qui taetri sanguinis acre   1205
exierat, tamen in nervos huic morbus et artus
ibat et in partis genitalis corporis ipsas.
et grauiter partim metuentes limina leti
uiuebant ferro priuati parte uirili,
et manibus sine non nulli pedibusque manebant   1210
in uita tamen et perdebant lumina partim.
usque adeo mortis metus iis incesserat acer.
atque etiam quosdam cepere obliuia rerum
cunctarum, neque se possent cognoscere ut ipsi.
multaque humi cum inhumata iacerent corpora supra   1215
corporibus, tamen alituum genus atque ferarum
aut procul absiliebat, ut acrem exiret odorem,
aut, ubi gustarat, languebat morte propinqua.
nec tamen omnino temere illis solibus ulla
comparebat auis, nec tristia saecla ferarum   1220
exibant siluis. languebant pleraque morbo
et moriebantur. cum primis fida canum uis
strata uiis animam ponebat in omnibus aegre;
extorquebat enim uitam uis morbida membris.
incomitata rapi certabant funera uasta   1225
nec ratio remedii communis certa dabatur;
nam quod ali dederat uitalis aëris auras
uoluere in ore licere et caeli templa tueri,
hoc aliis erat exitio letumque parabat.
illud in his rebus miserandum magnopere unum   1230
aerumnabile erat, quod ubi se quisque uidebat
implicitum morbo, morti damnatus ut esset,
deficiens animo maesto cum corde iacebat,
funera respectans animam amittebat ibidem.
quippe etenim nullo cessabant tempore apisci   1235
ex aliis alios auidi contagia morbi,
lanigeras tam quam pecudes et bucera saecla,

idque uel in primis cumulabat funere funus
nam qui cumque suos fugitabant uisere ad aegros,
uitai nimium cupidos mortisque timentis 1240
poenibat paulo post turpi morte malaque,
desertos, opis expertis, incuria mactans.
qui fuerant autem praesto, contagibus ibant
atque labore, pudor quem tum cogebat obire
blandaque lassorum uox mixta uoce querellae. 1245
optimus hoc leti genus ergo quisque subibat.
praeterea iam pastor et armentarius omnis
et robustus item curui moderator aratri
languebat, penitusque casa contrusa iacebant
corpora paupertate et morbo dedita morti. 1255
exanimis pueris super exanimata parentum
corpora non numquam posses retroque uidere
matribus et patribus natos super edere uitam.
nec minimam partem ex agris maeror is in urbem
confluxit, languens quem contulit agricolarum 1260
copia conueniens ex omni morbida parte.
omnia conplebant loca tectaque quo magis aestu,
confertos ita aceruatim mors accumulabat.
multa siti prostrata uiam per proque uoluta
corpora silanos ad aquarum strata iacebant 1265
interclusa anima nimia ab dulcedine aquarum,
multaque per populi passim loca prompta uiasque
languida semanimo cum corpore membra uideres
horrida paedore et pannis cooperta perire,
corporis inluuie, pelli super ossibus una, 1270
ulceribus taetris prope iam sordeque sepulta.
omnia denique sancta deum delubra replerat
corporibus mors exanimis onerataque passim
cuncta cadaueribus caelestum templa manebant,
hospitibus loca quae complerant aedituentes. 1275
nec iam religio diuom nec numina magni
pendebantur enim: praesens dolor exsuperabat.
nec mos ille sepulturae remanebat in urbe,
quo prius hic populus semper consuerat humari;
perturbatus enim totus trepidabat et unus 1280
quisque suum propere pro tempore maestus humabat.
multaque res subita et paupertas horrida suasit;

namque suos consanguineos aliena rogorum
insuper extructa ingenti clamore locabant
subdebantque faces, multo cum sanguine saepe   1285
rixantes, potius quam corpora desererentur,
inque aliis alium populum sepelire suorum   [1247]
certantes; lacrimis lassi luctuque redibant;   [1248]
inde bonam partem in lectum maerore dabantur;   [1249]
nec poterat quisquam reperiri, quem neque morbus   [1250]
nec mors nec luctus temptaret tempore tali.   [1251]

COMMENTARY

Book One

The poem begins with a prelude invoking the goddess Venus. This is one of the most surprising features of a surprising poem – for the poet frequently tells us that the gods do not listen to our prayers as they could not enjoy divine contentment if they were constantly being bothered by us. Many attempts have been made to explain this 'inconsistency' between the poet's theory and his practice which presents us with a picture of Venus embracing Mars and being asked to send peace to the troubled Romans.

One suggestion is that Venus here symbolises the 'force of nature' or vital energy which makes all things reproduce and brings into being the myriad life-forms we see. Venus is at once glossed as *hominum diuomque uoluptas* ('pleasure of men and gods') which reminds us that the Epicurean saw pleasure as the highest good: and the lavish colourful description of the world inspired by Venus shows us furthermore that the Epicurean view of the world is no cold grey place full of dull atoms but is the greatest show on earth. Now all these wondrous things are formed by atomic movements – but, at this point in the poem, it is important for the poet to show us how the pleasure of gazing at the world in all its variety mirrors the pleasure which he shows at work in reproducing life-forms and enjoying the world around us. This is to read the prelude as an allegory – but then that had been done of Aphrodite many times before both in poetry (see e.g. *Homeric Hymn to Aphrodite* 1-5, Euripides, *Hippolytus* 447-50) and also in philosophy (Empedocles frs. B17, 22, 35, 71, Parmenides B12.3-6 [DK]). This sort of metonymy is allowed later on by the poet (2. 655-60) provided that the reader refrains from 'polluting his mind with foul superstition'.

This allegorical interpretation is more difficult to sustain when Mars enters the picture, although the twin opposed forces of Love and Strife were at the heart of the universe according to Empedocles; however, if the poet intends us to read the passage in this symbolic way we might expect him to tell us so. A simpler reading is produced if we see these poetic images of the gods as being the sort of 'prayer' which the poet later on (6. 58-79) espouses as being likely to influence our behaviour and encourage us to emulate the *ataraxia* of the gods, so that here exchanging the 'image' of war for that of peace and creativity is good for all of us – the poet included who is here creating a poem.

The passage begins with the epic title *Aeneadum* and the poem is in the

25

tradition of didactic epic in which gods play an active part in the lives of men. It is conceivable that Lucretius writes in this 'epic' manner to hook his readers into a poem which will undermine the epic view of the world: a neat form of irony that uses poetry (which Epicurus famously disapproved of) to correct the 'poetic' view of the world, but which makes it clear throughout the text that removing false ideas about the world will not remove the colour and the pleasure from life. (For more discussion of this prelude see, for example, Godwin [1994] 244-50, Gale [1994] 208-23).

1   The first word of the first line places the text in the epic tradition. Aeneas was the Trojan prince, son of the goddess Venus and a mortal Anchises, and legendary founder of the Roman race after fleeing from the sack of Troy over the sea and landing in Italy – as described by Virgil in the *Aeneid*. Venus was the mother of Aeneas, who was the father of the Roman people, and so Venus is here addressed as 'mother of the sons of Aeneas'. The line goes on to describe the goddess as 'pleasure of men and gods', thus linking her with the Epicurean school which declared that pleasure was the highest good.

2   *alma* derives from *alo* ('I feed') and has the sense of 'nurturing'. Note how the name is only given in the second line. The 'signs of the heavens' are the stars: the poet ranges from sky to sea (*mare*) and earth (*terras*) in a sequence.

3   Note the poet's use of compound adjectives here and the repetition of the structure *quae* + noun + adjective, all of which imparts solemnity and weight to the line.

4   The verb *concelebras* is emphasised at the end of the phrase and the beginning of the line. The poet now begins a sequence of second person pronouns (*te...te...te...te...tibi...tibi*) which accentuate the apostrophe to the goddess appropriate to a hymn.

5   In crude mechanical terms, if Venus is the power of sexual love, then she is responsible for all mammalian reproduction; the poet expresses this more elegantly and poetically with the phrasing: the 'type of living things' is conceived and at once 'sees' the light of the sun: the three verbal forms *concipitur uisitque exortum* have a striking energy. For the phrase 'to see the light (of the sun)' meaning 'to live' cf. the parallel Greek phrase *phos blepein*.

6   Note the tricolon construction of three phrases each beginning with *te*.

7   *tuum tibi* is effective juxtaposition. *suauis* is here accusative plural agreeing with *flores* in the next line. *daedala* here means 'skilled' (cf. 5.234 below) and is usually applied to the works of human craftsmen: here the

	earth is personified as a skilled producer of flowers.
8	For the poetic notion of the sea 'laughing' cf. Catullus 31.14.
10	The key word here is *uerna*: it is in spring that mating and parturition happens, and so (as Venus is the goddess of sexual love) it must be Venus herself who is welcomed in the spring.
11	The metaphor in *reserata* is 'unlocked' and suggests the implicit myth of the winds locked in the cave of King Aeolus in Homer, *Odyssey* 10.21-2. The rest of the line emphasises the creative power of the wind: *uiget* suggests health, *genitabilis* suggests 'capable of giving life to'.
12	The poet repeats the apostrophe to the goddess with *diua* as before with *dea* in line 6. Note also the juxtaposition of *te diua tuumque* concentrating the terms of address.
13	*corda* is here accusative of respect: 'struck as to their hearts'. The monosyllabic ending to the line creates a bumpy rhythm which stresses the energy being described.
14	*ferae pecudes* is not to be taken together, as *fera* means a 'wild beast' while *pecudes* are herds of tame animals. The omission of 'and' is a device known as asyndeton and here suggests the rapid listing of types of animals all inspired by Venus, as well as imparting an archaic effect to the line. In this line and the next the poet again employs a varied sentence structure of verb-noun-adjective (*persultant pabula laeta*) followed by adjective-verb-noun (*rapidos tranant amnis*). *rapidus* has the obvious sense of 'rapid' but also suggests the verbal root *rapio* ('I snatch, seize') and thus here depicts the river in full flood carrying all with it – to swim across would require great effort. The vigour of the river is matched by the richness of the fields: *laeta* when applied to fields usually means 'rich, fruitful' but its common meaning of 'happy' is not out of place in the context of 'laughing' seas and leaping flocks. The poet also uses effective alliteration in *pecudes persultant pabula* and then strong assonance of *a* in *rapidos tranant amnis*.
15	*lepor* is a quality of elegance, charm: this is a surprising use of this word in the military metaphor of *capta...sequitur* suggesting that the hardness of war is captivated by the soft charms of Venus – a theme which the love of Mars and Venus at lines 29-40 will develop. In this sentence the subject of *sequitur* is *quaeque* ('each beast') supplied from *quamque*: 'thus captivated by your charm (each beast) follows you eagerly wherever you go on to lead each beast'.
16	Any actions induced by Venus will have quality of 'desire' in them and so *cupide* is no more than we expect – and the word is repeated at line 20.
17-18	The topography of animal life is itemised: seas and mountains are simply

referred to, but the poet then uses descriptive adjectives so that the rivers are *rapacis*, the trees are the 'leaf-bearing homes of birds' and the plains are 'green'. The impression created by this rapid tour is one of energy (*rapacis*), health (*uirentis*) and, above all, that beneath the surface of something as ordinary as a tree there is a world of life hidden – all couched in epic terminology.

19-20 If Venus strikes love into their hearts, then they will breed; this truism is made more impressive by the language used: *incutiens* is a violent word whereas *blandum* means 'coaxing, affectionate' (cf. 5.230 below), the juxtaposition producing an oxymoron which brings out both the force and the charm of Venus. Line 20 is framed by the verbs, with *cupide* appropriate to the acts of the mother of Cupid, and *generatim saecla* going well together.

21-7 The poet prays to Venus to assist his poem and names his addressee; since Venus alone 'steers' the *rerum naturam* then it is appropriate that she should also steer the poem *de rerum natura*. Later on the poet utters the more conventional address to the Muse Calliope (6. 92-5).

21 Note the (common) metaphor of steering a ship in *gubernas*.

22 *nec quicquam* means 'nor does anything'. The periphrasis 'arises into the bright shores of light' for 'is born' is a lively epic formula (cf. 5.224); the adjective *dias* is from *diuus* and has the primary sense 'bright' but a clear undertone of 'divine' – it is appropriate that a *diua* should produce living things into the *dias* shores of light.

23 Venus does not merely produce life but also joy and lovability, both of which will engender more life in their turn and (in the case of the poem) communicate to the reader this joy and love. Note how the two lines are framed by the parallel phrase *nec quicquam*.

24 *scribendis uersibus* is a dative of purpose after *sociam* ('a partner for the purpose of writing verses'). Note the heavy alliteration of 's' and the sense of *studeo* as 'I am keen for'.

25 This line signposts the title of the poem which is a Latin translation of the Greek *peri physeos*, the title of Empedocles' famous didactic poem and also a prose treatise of Epicurus. *pangere* properly means 'to construct' and suggests the building of a house; there is a touch of modesty in *conor* which fits well with the prayer to the goddess.

26 Gaius Memmius was an important man in the politics of the late Roman Republic and a literary dilettante (Ovid, *Tristia* 2.433) who was as well known for his political ambition as his furious sex-drive (he even tried to seduce the wife of Pompey the Great) – a perfect candidate for Epicurean conversion. (On this topic, see Godwin [1994] 251-4.) Here the poet uses the elegant patronymic form 'to the scion of Memmius' for the unmetrical *Memmio* and at once claims him as his own (*nostro*).

26-7 The remark that Venus wanted Memmius to excel in all things is interesting. On the one hand, the coins of the Memmii of the Galeria tribe have the goddess Venus on them and so she may be the family patroness; on the other hand his sexual appetites were so legendary that the poet may here be alluding to his devotion to Venus 'at all times'. Notice here the polyptoton of *omni omnibus* over the line-break in fulsome praise of Memmius, and the rhetorical term *ornatum* (see OLD s.v. 'orno' 4c,5) used of the political animal himself.

28 The prayer sums up: Venus should be 'all the more' willing to assist as Memmius is her favourite. Most surprising is the poet's wish for 'eternal' grace to be given to the poem as he frequently tells us how we ourselves will die and the world with us. Note here the sequence of alliterative words *da dictis diua* and the final juxtaposition of *diua leporem* indicative of the way in which she is the source of *lepos* (15) and lovability (23).

29-49 The mythology becomes more involved as the poet now invokes the goddess for peace, drawing on the traditional imagery of her love-affair with the god of war (Mars) and the topical allusion to Memmius' political involvement.

29-30 Earlier on Venus was credited with awakening all living things to life and breeding, now she is credited with the reverse power to send to sleep the 'wild works of warfare' (Bailey) 'through seas and all lands'. *moenus* is an archaic form of the noun *munus* meaning 'task, drill' and also 'duty' and even 'gladiatorial show'. The genitive ending *-ai* is an archaic feature which Lucretius adopts frequently in the poem. *sopita quiescant* is an emphatic juxtaposition.

31 Venus is divine, and gods enjoy tranquillity (3. 18-24) and so it is apt that Venus can send this tranquillity, except that the need to send tranquillity would itself disturb the divine serenity.

32 *belli fera moenera* recalls line 29 and sets up the alliteration of *moenera Mauors*, the name (for Mars) being both archaic and suggestive of the word *mors* ('death') and also framing the line which began with *mortalis*.

32-4 Mars rules war – but Venus rules over Mars, and so Venus can rule over war. *armipotens* is a grand compound adjective for a grand warrior-god who 'rules' (*regit*) even what is 'savage' (*fera*). The grandeur is however soon dissipated as the war-god throws himself into the lap of Venus, the verbal juxtaposition of *tuum se* bringing their embrace to life. This happens 'often' and his love is an 'eternal' wound.

34   There is nice irony here in the conqueror being conquered, the wounds inflicted on this warrior being those of love and not war. For the imagery of love as warfare cf. Ovid, *Amores* 1.9: for the tale of how Mars (Ares) was seduced by Venus (Aphrodite) and then caught and humiliated by her husband Mulciber (Hephaestus) see Homer, *Odyssey* 8.266-369.

35-40   The poet describes the scene in lavish detail, concentrating on how Venus is above Mars and dominant over him. The description of the scene suggests the composition of a work of art.

35   *tereti ceruice reposta* is an ablative absolute construction, with *reposta* a contracted form of *reposita*. Mars' neck is *teres*, 'rounded' and even 'shapely' (M.F. Smith).

36   The imagery here is striking: Mars 'feeds, gasping, his greedy eyes with love', with *auidos* and *inhians* juxtaposed for effect. The metaphor 'feeds' is later on developed when the poet urges that (unlike hunger and thirst) our sex-drive is a quest for empty images which can never satisfy (see 4.1091-6 below). If Mars really can 'feed' on love, then he is luckier than mere mortals. The broken rhythm of *te dea uisus* – with the word stress falling (unusually) on the second syllable of the fifth foot – may perhaps suggest the panting of the amorous god.

37   The close contact of the gods is beautifully brought out by the breathing of the god 'hanging' from the mouth of the goddess (*spiritus ore* juxta-posed verbally as in life) as he lies back on her lap (*resupini*). The word *spiritus* is apt here, meaning both 'breathing' and 'imperious disposi-tion' (OLD s.v. 'spiritus' 7d) while *pendet* means 'hangs from' but also 'droops' (OLD s.v. 'pendeo' 5b): and so the whole sentence well captures the sense of the god of war losing his warlike spirit in face of Venus.

38   Mars is the short word *hunc* overpowered verbally by the concatenation of *tu diua tuo* as he lies on her *corpore sancto* by which she is '*circumfusa*' about him – the ablative term going with both participles. *sanctus* is an interesting choice of word: as applied to a goddess it means primarily 'divine, holy' but also has the sense 'pure, chaste' (OLD s.v. 'sanctus' 4c) and 'untouchable, inviolate'.

39   *suauis* agrees with *loquellas*: the term *loquella* is later used (5. 230) of the cooing blandishments of the nurse trying to get the baby to eat. *ex ore* is no empty padding: it recalls line 37 and stresses that (if Mars is hanging from her mouth) then she should seize this captive audience.

40   Note that Venus is *circumfusa* and is now told to *funde*, the imperative followed by *petens* which functions as another command. She is addressed as *incluta*, as is Epicurus in 3.10 and Memmius at 5.8. *placidam...pacem* might seem something of a tautology but, apart from the 'p' alliteration,

it affords a greater emphasis on the quiet and peace being sought which sounds very close to the *ataraxia* (serenity) which for Epicurus was the highest good.

41 *agere hoc* is a vague phrase meaning 'do my part' (M.F. Smith). The metaphor of *iniquo* (see OLD s.v. 'iniquus' 6c) as 'stormy' creates a vivid picture: and 'at this stormy period for our fatherland' suggests that the lines were being written in the period leading up to the civil war (49-45 BC) – but Memmius' finest political hour was probably his praetorship in 58 BC, a year which saw the tribunate of Publius Clodius and gang-warfare on the streets. (For an account of this period see, for example, Syme [1939] ch.3.)

42 The adjective *aequo* picks up *iniquo* from the previous line and produces something of a *petitio principii* (if things are not *aequus*, then we cannot have an *aequus* mind) and reflects 'the inevitable connection between political and mental turmoil' (Brown [1984] 51). The phrasing *Memmi clara propago* ('the noble offspring of Memmius') suggests a policy of *noblesse oblige* whereby so distinguished a citizen has to get involved in his country's turmoil.

43 *communi..saluti* sounds like espousal of the republican cause against the threat of tyranny (see Griffin [1989] 30) which would fit the anti-Caesarian feeling in the 50s BC. Epicureanism was notoriously apolitical, although the wise man might act to preserve social safety (see Fowler [1989]). The sentence as a whole is praise of the addressee (as indispensable to his country) but does not sit well with the traditionally apolitical stance of the Epicureanism towards which the text is leading him; Memmius, far from giving up politics, is needed more than ever.

44-9 These lines recur in 2.646-51 and fit badly into the context here: some editors (e.g. Bailey's OCT and Brown) omit the lines entirely, others print them with misgivings and doubts (e.g. Bailey's 1947 edition, and Smith). It is arguable that they were first composed for their place in Book 2 and moved here to be shaped into a passage 'correcting' the false theology of the prelude. It is even possible that a scribe, aware of the inconsistency between the prayer and the Epicurean view of the gods, transferred the lines here (as argued by Voss). If they were placed here by the poet, the connection of thought must be: 'give the Romans peace, for the gods enjoy unbroken peace'. Venus has been invoked to grant peace to Rome, and the poet now explains the sort of peace which the Gods enjoy: the passage thus functions as a contrast to the troubled times of Rome and a paradigm of the sort of peace which is being sought.

44-5 Gods, by definition, enjoy deathless time and the utmost peace.

46	This is the major area of conflict with what has preceded: if the gods are removed *nostris ab rebus* then why should Venus assist Rome and the poet now? Note here the duplication of *semota...seiunctaque*.
47	A rhetorical line using fine anaphora of *priuata* and alliteration of 'p'.
49	The two usual expectations of gods are that they will reward good deeds and punish the wicked; Lucretius assures us that neither is the case.
50-61	The poet outlines the syllabus of subject matter: the poet will explain the atoms. The first four lines express concern that the reader will dismiss the subject matter before it is understood.
50	*quod superest* simply means 'next' and occurs frequently in Lucretius. The mind of the reader must be 'sharp'.
51	*semotum a curis* is both good sense – it is no use trying to read philosophy when your mind is on other things and the reader must be 'unpreoccupied' (Brown's translation of *uacuas*) – and very good Epicureanism, as Epicurus prized *ataraxia* ('freedom from worry, serenity') as the height of happiness.
52-3	The metaphor is possibly that of a banquet (as Brown [1984] suggests) which Memmius is not to scorn before he has grasped the goods on offer. The word order in 53 is also expressive: *intellecta* is put outside its clause and balanced against *contempta*, with the juxtaposition of 'contempt' and 'abandon' in *contempta relinquas* forming a weighty conclusion to the line.
54-61	Lucretius lays out the enticing material to be served: the reader is promised the truth about the sky, the gods and the atoms. Note how he attempts to tempt the reader with big claims of what is to be told. The *ratio* of the sky is *summa*, he will talk of the gods and he will show the atoms from which nature makes 'all things' as well as explaining death (57). The paragraph concludes with some enticing technical language to convince the reader that he will learn something here from a poet who is an authority on the subject. It is interesting that he hooks the reader with astronomy and meteorology (which the poem will not discuss until the last two books), and only then mentions the atomic theory which will occupy much of the first two books. The syllabus for Books 3 and 4 will not appear until lines 131-5.
54	Lucretius deals with the sky and its phenomena in Book 6, having covered astronomy in Book 5.
55	The line is framed by the two important verbs *disserere* and *pandam*. The *rerum primordia* are the 'first-beginnings of things' or the atoms.
56	Nature is personified as the creator and then the 'dissolver' of 'things' – and later on speaks to rebuke the man reluctant to die (3. 931-77) –

but this does not imply that Lucretius believed that there was a personal deity at work creating the world as we see it. Note here the three verbs *creet...auctet alatque* for the threefold activity of creating, making to grow and then feeding.

57 Nature makes things grow and break up once again (*rursum*) into their constituent atoms when they are destroyed: the poet here is drawing attention to the way in which things come into being and then die, but the atoms of which they are made are eternal.

58-61 The poet lists some of the various synonyms for 'atoms' in Latin: *materiem* (literally = 'matter'), *genitalia corpora* ('bodies which give life'), *semina rerum* ('the seeds of things') and *corpora prima* ('first bodies'), while at the same time finding synonyms for the verb 'to call' (*uocare, appellare, usurpare*) and finishing off with a fine rhetorical line with epanalepsis of *prima...primis*.

58 The word *materiem* sounds as if it has *mater* ('mother': cf. 170-1) in it and leads well onto *genitalia* and then *semina*.

59 *reddere rationem* is properly to 'render an account' (see OLD s.v. 'reddo' 13b) and is a financial term.

60 The two synonymous words for 'call' frame the line: *suemus* is scanned as three syllables.

61 The line makes better sound than sense: the epanalepsis of *prima...primis* is rhetorically effective but the meaning is (at this point in the poem) elusive and will await further explanation later on as the poet will show how 'things' (*rerum*) are made up of atoms.

62-79 Praise of Epicurus, especially for his subjugation of religion. Books 3, 5 and 6 all similarly open with praise of Epicurus. The picture of human life grovelling under fear and superstition is intended to highlight the achievement of Epicurus.

62 *ante oculos* means here 'for all to see'. The metaphor of 'lying prostrate' to indicate a state of degradation (OLD s.v. 'iaceo' 3a) furthers the spatial metaphor whereby religion is towering above mortal men until Epicurus 'dared to raise his eyes'.

63 The plural *terris* indicates that it was not merely Greece which suffered but all nations. *religio* here means 'religious fear' as a source of fear, rather than the 'true religion' (which Lucretius discusses at 6.68-79) that can inspire men to a life of 'divine' *ataraxia*. The final five-syllable word *religione* 'weighs down the line, as if mirroring *religio*'s effect on mankind' (Brown [1984] 55). The imagery of weight is unremitting in the juxtaposition of *graui oppressa*.

64 Lucretius plays on the words for religion: *religio* came down from the *caeli regionibus*, while *superstitio* was the force which was *super instans*. Religion here is a monster lowering down from the clouds – apt as for most people their fear of gods was born of their incomprehension of meteorological phenomena, and so the imagery of divine heads in the sky with dreadful gaze is no empty poetic conceit. Note the heavy, threatening slowness of the fifth-foot spondee *ostendebat*.

66   *mortalis* is accusative agreeing with *oculos* in the next line but effectively juxtaposed here with *homo*. Epicurus' achievement is stressed by the repetition *primum...primusque*: his fame is such that the poet does not need to name him here (in fact he is only named once, at 3.1042) but there is also something extra special about this man who was, after all, just a 'Greek man' taking on the might of the gods. The struggle of Epicurus against the gods is emphasised by the repetition of *contra* at the end of two consecutive lines.

68-9   Epicurus was not scared either by the stories of the gods or the thunderbolts in the sky. The lines have a fine alliterative rhetoric to them: *neque fama...nec fulmina: minitanti murmure compressit caelum*; and note the vigorous syncopation of *eo magis acrem*. The verb *compressit* continues the imagery of *oppressa* from line 63 and contrasts the behaviour of Epicurus with that of everybody else.

70-9   The imagery of military conquest now becomes prominent as Epicurus showed his *uirtus*, shattered the bolts of the gates of nature, marched forth and brought back victory over religion.

70   The third syllable of *inritat* is long as the word is a contraction of *inritauit*. The locks on the gates of nature are *arta* and his shattering of them employs alliteration of 'p' and 'c'. The phrasing might lead the reader to think that nature was the enemy, whereas it is *religio* which will be defeated when the secrets of nature are unlocked. Nature is the treasure which Epicurus has wrested from the enemy Religion.

71   Once again the poet stresses the priority of Epicurus (*primus*) even though he was but one in a long line of Greek philosophers who sought and helped to find the truth about Nature. The atomic theory was first invented by Democritus and Leucippus well over a century before Epicurus.

72   The rhetoric continues with repetition of consonantal 'u' and assonance of 'i'. The line runs onto line 73 suggestive of the onward march of Epicurus.

73   The 'flaming walls of the world' refers to the ether which surrounds our world and is literally a wall of fire. At this point in the poem the reader is not expected to understand the cosmology but will be impressed by the

74   imagery of the daring of a general who marched even through walls of fire.

74   Epicurus roamed through the whole universe – in his mind. The last two words, far from underplaying the victory, make his achievement even more impressive. Simply by the power of his mind he could do all this: cf. how later Epicurus' *dicta* are seen as superior to the *arma* of Hercules (5.50 below). *omne* means 'the universe' while *immensum* looks forward to the discussion of the infinity of the universe (1.921-1007).

75   Epicurus brought back the spoils of his campaign; but his spoils consist in factual propositions about the limitations of matter and the universe. 'What can arise and what cannot' is of course very much to the point in the victory over superstition, which frightens us with things that cannot exist anyway – monsters, the torments of the dead, and so on.

77   The 'deepset boundary stone' marking the edge of a property appears several times in the poem (1.595-6, 5.89-90, 6.65-6) and gives the passage a legalistic and Roman tone. Here, the victorious general might be expected to set up a 'trophy' to mark his victory but this general set up a stone showing the limits of nature. In Roman religion, the god of the boundary-stone (Terminus) is said to have refused to give way to Jupiter Optimus Maximus when a temple was being built for the latter on the Capitol and remained stubbornly in place (see OCD s.v. 'Terminus') – *alte terminus haerens* indeed.

78-9   The lines refer back to the beginning of the passage where religion had mortal men under foot; the tables are turned (*uicissim*) and we now crush religion. *uictoria* picks up *uictor* in line 75. The image in the final phrase is complex: Epicurus investigated the sky and so his victory brings us to the scene of his triumph and his victory also makes us equal to the gods.

80-101 The rejection of religion has often been seen as offering a licence to be immoral; Lucretius counters this by showing that it is more often religion which produces wicked behaviour and cites the famous example of human sacrifice from the start of the Trojan War.

81   The word *impia* is stressed at the beginning of the line; note also the sardonic metaphor 'walking upon the path of crime', which is very much the sort of moralising metaphor that might be used against (the supposedly atheist and immoral) Epicurean.

83   The metaphor in *peperit* is of giving birth (from *pario*).

84-101 The tale of Iphigeneia is well known: the Greek fleet on the way to Troy was becalmed at Aulis in Boeotia owing to the hostility of the goddess Artemis, and so the Greek leader Agamemnon summoned his daughter

Iphigeneia on the false pretext that she was to marry Achilles and then sacrificed her to placate the goddess. The example of a legendary tale here is somewhat odd when the poet might have been better to choose, say, the human sacrifice before the battle of Salamis as recorded by Plutarch (*Themistocles* 13) which had the advantage of being from a 'real' war. The slaughter of a mythical virgin before a legendary war does not, it might be urged, have the same contemporary power to persuade Roman readers to change their (Roman) behaviour. The advantage of the tale of Iphigeneia here is that it is well known to the Roman reader from the accounts in Greek Tragedy (Aeschylus, *Agamemnon* and Euripides, *Iphigeneia at Aulis*, for instance) and so carries an emotional 'charge' which the poet can tune into – a sort of persuasive short-cut. There is a further possibility that this passage is a description of a famous painting of the sacrifice of Iphigeneia, which Cicero (*Orator* 74) tells us of.

84 The goddess *Triuia* is the goddess 'Diana of the crossroads', the Roman equivalent of the Greek goddess Artemis, to whom Iphigeneia was sacrificed. *quo pacto* means 'just as'; the word *uirginis* is pointed – a virgin was offered to a virgin, and the word *uirginis* might (grammatically) be taken either with *Triuiai* or with *Iphianassai*.

85 *turparunt* (= *turpauerunt*) is strongly pejorative: the leaders of the Greeks were doing what they thought was the right thing but it was a 'befouling' of the altar. This is all the more surprising when the fouling was done with blood – as that was what altars were for – but not the blood of one's own child. *Iphianassa* is an alternative form of 'Iphigeneia' here; other writers (e.g. *Cypria* frag. 15) tell us that Agamemnon had four daughters, with Iphianassa being a sister of Iphigeneia who outlived her (cf. Homer, *Iliad* 9. 145; Sophocles, *Electra* 158) but there is no suggestion anywhere that it was this Iphianassa who was killed by her father.

86 Note the grandiose phrasing with its pompous alliteration of 'd' and heavy sarcasm in 'first of men'. After the panegyric of the 'general-ship' of Epicurus in the previous section, these Greek generals are meant to sound very much second-rate.

87 The *infula* was the ribbon of twisted wool worn by sacrificial victims in Roman ritual; Iphigeneia was expecting the hairband (*uitta*) of the bride which would be appropriate to her 'virginal tresses'. The accusative *comptus* is governed by the *circum* in *circumdata* ('put around her hair').

88 The ribbon fell down her cheeks evenly on both sides: 'the elaborate precision of the ceremonial is in sharp contrast with the primitive barbarity of the deed itself' (Brown [1984] 61).

89   The 'sad parent' frames this line whose sadness is brought out by the assonance of 'a' throughout.

90   Note the stress on *sensit* at the start of the line and end of the phrase. *hunc propter* means 'next to this man'. The servants are hiding the weapon but she has already seen this (*sensit*) and so their efforts to spare her fears are in vain.

91   The theme of sadness continues: not only the father but the 'citizens' are now weeping – by which is meant the Greek soldiers or else the citizens of Aulis itself. *aspectu suo* means 'at the sight of her' but also carries the sense of 'at the look on her face' (OLD s.v. 'aspectus' 4b): just as Iphigeneia was seen to see (*sensit*) earlier on, we now see others seeing her – and seeing the look on her face.

92   *muta metu* is a fine phrase both for sound and also sense as her fear makes her speechless and it is her limbs which act ('let down by her knees she sank to the ground').

93-4   Her status as her father's first child did her no good at all (cf. Aeschylus, *Agamemnon* 228-30). *in tali tempore* recalls lines 41 and 43: the construction is 'she had been the first to endow (*donarat*) the king with the name of father', as urged by Iphigeneia in Euripides (*I.A.* 1220). The scorn in the words is brought out by the spitting 'p' alliteration of *patrio princeps* and also the faint undertone of 'chief' in *princeps* which applies to Agamemnon more than to the helpless victim. The clash of roles is well remembered by Ovid (*Metamorphoses* 12.30) who puts the situation concisely: *rexque patrem uicit*.

95   Her helplessness is brought out by the way in which she is carried by the hands of (nameless) men to the altars – a notion imitative of Aeschylus, *Agamemnon* 231-3.

96   *deductio* was the technical term for the entry of the bride into her new husband's home (Treggiari [1991] 166) which was the sort of *deductio* that Iphigeneia was expecting; here the term *deducta* is used sardonically of her being led to her death. The contrast between the marriage and her execution is now explicitly emphasised by the poet in sneering terms. *solemni more sacrorum* is somewhat vague ('in the time-honoured manner of sacred rites') and could as well describe either a sacrifice or a wedding.

97   The alliteration is obvious here of 'p' and 'c'. The wedding terminology is left until the end of the line: *Hymenaeus* was the title of the formal wedding song, which had the customary refrain 'Hymenaeus' addressing the god Hymen (child of the Muse Urania; see Godwin [1995] 102) who was the god of weddings. *claro* here means 'loud'.

98   The oxymoron of *casta inceste* is pointed; and the mention of *nubendi* is unnecessary but allows the poet to stress both the girl's youth and also the deception required to arrange her presence.

99   *maesta* is perhaps an understatement but recalls *maestum* used of Agamemnon at line 89. To bring out the barbarism of the deed, Lucretius has Agamemnon perform the killing himself (cf. Euripides, *I.A.* 1178, but see also 1578-9, where it is open to question who did the killing). The terms *hostia concideret* are correct for an animal sacrifice (see, for example, 2.353 below) but icily cold here for a parent to do to his child, as brought out by the postponement of *parentis* to the end of the line.

100   The inadequate reason for the sacrifice is stated bluntly with strong emphasis on the juxtaposed near-synonyms *felix faustusque* (it was hardly *felix* for Iphigeneia), which in turn contrast with the word *maesta* in the previous line.

101   The conclusion of the accumulated evidence of the preceding twenty lines is clear and refers us back to the point with which this passage began (80): if you think *ratio* is immoral, just look at what *religio* has done. The word *suadere* is well chosen as religious ideas do not 'force' us to kill our daughters but they 'persuade' us to do so if we listen to them.

The next passage is a declaration of intent and an apologia for writing verse. Lines 926-50 are also to be found at 4.1-25; the poet repeats whole passages in this way several times (cf. 3.806-18 = 5.351-63; 1.1021-7 = 5.419-29) rather in the manner of Homer, and editors have often sought to place the passage as more appropriate in one place rather than another – a fruitless quest in this case, as the passage was read in both books in antiquity and there is no evidence that the poet did not intend it to be so read.

Two ideas are interwoven into the passage. Firstly, the originality of Lucretius' enterprise, and, secondly, its purpose. The argument of the text suggests that the poetry is only of secondary importance to the message being propounded, and yet this 'mission' is only declared after nine lines charged with Alexandrian allusions declaring the poet's hopes of achieving poetic glory and originality. The sequence of thought thus teases the reader with the language of Alexandrian hermetic, obscure poetics announcing a very un-Alexandrian public mission which totally subverts the poetry to a purpose outside of itself. The poem *is* original – and it is a technical *tour de force* to turn difficult philosophy into delightful poetry – and yet its originality rests at least partly on its refusal to espouse the Alexandrian poetic of 'art for art's sake'.

921   *clarius* is positioned to contrast with *obscura* in the next line, the 'brightness' in *clarius* contrasted with the darkness in *obscura*.

923   The *thyrsus* was the staff wielded by the devotees of Bacchus; it was wound with ivy and vine-shoots and had the power to cause water to flow from the bare rock (Euripides, *Bacchae* 704-5), just as the poet seeks springs of poetic inspiration in 927-8. The *thyrsus* could also cause madness (Horace, *Odes* 2.19.8, with Nisbet and Hubbard *ad loc*; Dodds [1960] 82) and is here seen as the metaphor for poetic inspiration. There is something of a paradox in the Epicurean (whose motto was 'live unknown' and who mocks those who die 'for the sake of statues and a name' [3.78]) seeking 'praise', although one might urge that the praise will be merely an indicator of the poetic success which will *s*pread the creed rather than the empty pursuit of fame. Note how the percussive action of the *thyrsus* (brought out in the twin verbs *percussit...incussit*) is matched by the vigorous syncopation of *magna meum cor* at the end of the line.

924   There is a striking oxymoron in the violent verb *incussit* being used of *suauem...amorem*.

925   The poet has addressed the goddess Venus as his *sociam* in the prelude to the poem, but later on he invokes the Muse Calliope (6.92-5). The Muses were traditionally the nine sisters who inspired artists and poets.

926   The collocation of *auia Pieridum* stresses that it is artistic originality to which the poet lays claim: in his philosophy he is a faithful disciple of Epicurus, but in his poetry he is his own master.

      The Muses were called *Pierides* from their assocation with Mount Pierus in Thessaly.

927   An old tradition associates water with poetry and the motifs of untraversed paths and untouched springs are particularly reminiscent of Callimachus.

929-30   'The notion of crowning by the Muses recalls the tradition of symbolic gift-giving that began with Hesiod (*Theogony* 30-1) and was continued by Theocritus...' (Kenney [1970a] 371). The poet has already described how Ennius 'was the first to bring down from lovely Helicon a crown of evergreen leafage' (1.117-18), words which are charged with reminiscence of the proem of Ennius' *Annales*. Lucretius provocatively asserts his originality in words which are anything but original, alluding to the encomium which the poet traditionally bequeathes to his subject and then (as it were) setting the crown on his own head as poet.

931-2   This poetry is going to be therapeutic and rid us of unhealthy religious fears, which it has been his purpose to eliminate right from the beginning (cf. 1. 63-5, 80-101 above).

932   The poet plays on the word *religio* as being derived from *religare*

('bind'). See West (1969) 96.

933   In the prelude to Book 3 (1-2) Lucretius describes Epicurus as raising so bright a light in such darkness. Light is used as a symbol of poetic clarity as also of philosophical truth dispelling the shadows of ignorance and fear.

934   Note the alliteration of *c* in *carmina contingens cuncta* and the vocalic richness of *musaeo contingens cuncta* – all five vowels and a diphthong in three words.

935   What West (1969) calls the 'brutal prosiness of this line' is especially striking after the poetic riches of lines 926-34 and yet part of Lucretius' virtuosity is precisely his ability to create poetry out of whatever comes to hand, and his refusal to allow notions of poetic propriety to deflect him from the directness which he seeks.

936-42   Lucretius outlines what has been called 'the ornamental or seductive theory of art'. (Arragon, 371). The unconverted are compared to sick children who have to be tricked into taking unpleasant medicine (for the analogy cf. Plato, *Laws* 659e-660a, Horace, *Satires* 1.1.25-6). The analogy is powerful, in that it reduces opponents to the status of children, it suggests that the poet has a role comparable to that of the doctor treating a patient, and it also emphasises the primacy of contact as the source of true perception – a notion which Book 4 takes pains to prove. The literary implications of the passage are wide indeed. There is a clear allusion to the old tradition of poetry being between truth and fiction, the two being indistinguishable to the poet and his audience (Hesiod, *Theogony* 26-8, Solon 21, Pindar, *Olympian* 1.21f, *Nemean* 7.20ff, Euripides, *Heracles* 1341-6, Callimachus, *Hymn* 1. 5-8) while these same poets may assert the truth of their words no less firmly than Lucretius does here (Hesiod, *Works and Days* 10, Pindar, *Olympian* 13.52, Callimachus frag. 442). Lucretius transforms this idea into the paradox that the deliberate use of deceit is necessary to tell the truth.

    The mixture of honey and wormwood is compared with the union of sour philosophy and sweet poetry in a novel variation of the claim to produce work which is both 'sweet and useful' (*dulce et utile*). In Book 6 we will see the reverse, as the philosophy of Epicureanism will sweeten the impact of the unpleasant message conveyed by the poetry in telling of the plague in Athens.

936   Wormwood was used in the treatment of pain in throat and stomach.

937   Giving medicine to children is not easy, as is brought out by the verb *conantur* and the plural *pocula.* In lines 948-9 the poet is similarly trying to engage the reader.

938   This mirrors line 934: *contingens...lepore* becoming *contingunt liquore.* 'The smooth "l" sounds fit the sweetness of the honey, the slow rhythm its viscosity' (Brown). Note also how the poet brings out the importance of the colour of the liquid (yellow) in persuading the child to drink it.

939-40   There is a neat irony here: one would expect the child to be playing a prank on adults rather than vice versa. *perpotet* has the sense of 'carouse' and thus adds a comic touch of the child being drunk on wormwood (cf. 1.260-1, West [1969] 6-7).

941   For the play on words which creates the jingle *deceptaque non capiatur* cf. Ennius, *Annales* 359, Virgil, *Aeneid* 7.295. The phrase – which relies on the fact that the one word is derived from the other – produces a paradox: even though the child is *decepta* he is not *capiatur*.

942   The manuscripts read *atacto* and most modern editors emend this to *pacto*: I have printed the reading of Lambinus *tactu* which is allitera- tively pleasing and also stresses the key concept of physical contact – one of the main themes running through the whole of Book 4. All sensation, Lucretius argues, is a matter of contact (2.434-5), even sight being the result of the impact of images (*simulacra*) on the eyes.

      The term *ualescat* is interesting: the unconverted are compared to the sick, just as later on the romantic lover is *saucius* (wounded), his love a fever (*rabies*). The fear of death makes man sick with sorrow (3.933-4), just as religion crushes him prostrate (1.62-3). The climax of this theme of sickness is of course the lengthy description of the plague at Athens with which the poem ends.

944   *tristis* is used elsewhere of noxious smells (4.125) and unpleasant food (4.634), thus neatly overlapping the sense of bitter medicine and the emotionally unattractive features of Epicureanism.

945   A few years later Cicero speaks of Epicureanism 'taking over the whole of Italy' (*Tusculan Disputations* 4.6-7), particularly among the unedu- cated who knew no better. Epicureanism had been known in Italy at least since 154 BC and reached a peak of popularity in the late Republic, its apolitical stance perhaps appealing to the people disillusioned with the political scene. It may be that Lucretius is here exaggerating the unpopularity of Epicureanism for two reasons: firstly, Epicurus himself claimed never to have sought to please the masses (Usener 187); and secondly, the sentiment puts the poet and his audience on a higher intel- lectual plane and flatters them (cf. Horace, *Odes* 3.1.1, Williams 49f).

946   Pierio recalls *Pieridum* from line 926, just as *contingere melle* recalls line 934, a clear example of ring-composition which signals that the passage is drawing to its close.

Book Two

The book begins with the word *suaue* (pleasant) and reminds the reader that pleasure is for the Epicurean the highest good. The pleasure here is analysed as follows:

1)   1-19 Personal pleasure is found in watching the sufferings and toils of others from a safe contemplative distance and seeing that such striving is quite unnecessary.

2)   20-36 Luxury is no benefit to the body; and nature provides what we need free of all effort.

3)   37-61 The mind also does not need luxuries, and the show of military power does not succeed in ridding us of unhealthy fears which themselves fear no show of might; only philosophy can rid us of these fears.

The moral tone in this passage is apparently one simply of enlightened self-interest and disillusion with the conventional icons of success and happiness, such as the proverbial *adikos eudaimon* ('wicked but happy') tyrant figure found in, for example, Plato, *Gorgias* 470c9-471d2; the rich and powerful are not for that reason happy, while the poor and powerless may be happy with the aid of reason. The world is not a perfect place, but we can all be happy in it. The philosopher will not take part in politics as the bear-garden of politics is too rough and dangerous for peace of mind and he can (and should) shelter from the storm, as suggested by Socrates in Plato's *Republic* 496d. Lucretius even suggests that the politically powerful are in fact weaker than the non-political sage. The passage is thus in 'political' terms something of an exercise in turning the tables on the powerful of the world, whereby their show of power (notice for instance how the legions evoke only the *simulacra* of war [41], a remark justifiable in Epicureanism but here of obvious satirical force) is a mere show with no substance, while the reality behind the façade is one of fear and impotence in the face of nature, death, religion and so on – a situation later memorably described by Horace, *Odes* 3.1.34-40. The rich and powerful are theatrical in their elaborate costume and decor (notice how the poet treats us to a lavish verbal description of the luxurious house redolent of Homer's palace on Scheria), but behind the trappings they are as weak as the rest of us, their costumes a mere façade of empty appearance. When a rich man and a poor man are sick, the expensive bedclothes of the former give him no advantage over the latter, whereas the wise man is always superior to the fool in being free from the mental pains of fear and superstition. Once again there is theatrical irony here: the wise man is the audience who sees the spectacle enacted by the fools and derives safe aesthetic pleasure from the displayed actions, while being aware that the spectacle is no more than an empty show of inane fatuity. The fool, on the other hand, is in fact on the stage acting out a futile role but believes that he is 'really' pursuing pleasure and happiness in his quest for power and wealth: he is an actor unaware of his role. The wise man does not enjoy the suffering of the fool because he likes people to be hurt – why, in that case, would the poem affect to convert the fools to a happier state of mind if by doing so it would reduce the amount of folly available for our entertainment? Rather the poem presents the inescapable fact of the contrast between wisdom and folly, between action and contemplation, between sure aesthetic pleasure and futile seeking after pleasure through power and greed.

The passage has often been seen as ethically and morally somewhat distasteful. Bailey ([1947] 797) asserts that the lines

> have an unpleasant taste of egoism and even of cruelty. The Epicurean philosopher, secure in his own independence, gazing on the troubles and struggles of his fellow-men is an almost cynical picture; Bacon referred to it ironically as 'Lucretian pleasure'.

The prevailing attitude appears egotistical and it is hard to defend Lucretius against this charge. Nor can we excuse the poet on the grounds that these are post-Christian sensitivities not shared by the ancients: Aristotle (*Nicomachean Ethics* 1107a10) regards *epichairekakia* (rejoicing at the misfortunes of others) as an unmitigated evil which does not allow of a 'golden mean' and links it with adultery, theft and murder.

This is, however, to misunderstand the literary tradition in which this passage is composed. In the first place it is one of respectable atomist ancestry: the atomist philosopher Democritus expresses a very similar view when he says: 'one should look at those in trouble, being aware of how they badly are suffering. This way what you have will seem great and enviable to you' (Frag. 594 KRS).

The urge towards *Schadenfreude* (rejoicing in the misfortune of others) is perhaps not one which people would readily admit to; but for Epicurus there is no court of appeal beyond the provision of pleasure to the individual: 'strictly speaking there is no concept of moral obligation or of moral evil in Epicureanism' (Rist [1972] 125) and so the primacy of pleasure justifies the laughter for the Epicurean without any further ado. There is inevitably an element of such superiority in any philosophical or religious system which promises to elevate the wise man or the initiated above his peers into the realms of blessedness, and Lucretius is simply (in this, as in much else) being more honest about it.

There are then other distinguished ancients who subscribe to Lucretius' enjoyment of others' suffering: Cicero is explicit and interesting on the whole topic in seeking Lucceius' favourable report of his political career:

My own misfortunes will provide you with great variety of material, full of a sort of pleasure which could grip the mind of the readers so long as you are the author. For there is nothing more fitted to please the reader than the changes of time and the ups and downs of fortune; I did not choose them to live through but they will be pleasurable in the reading – for the safe recollection of pain from the past does give delight. And everyone else – who have not lived through sorrows of their own but who look upon the misfortunes of others without any pain – finds their pity a source of pleasure.... A list of events in chronological order only holds our attention to a moderate extent...but the uncertain and varied fortunes of a pre-eminent man bring out wonder, suspense, joy, pain, hope, fear: and if they are rounded off with a famous death, then the mind is filled full with the sweetest reading pleasure.   (*ad Fam.* 5.12.4-5)

Shackleton-Bailey ([1965] 367) cites some interesting Epicurean lines from Tibullus:

> quam iuuat immites uentos audire cubantem
>   et dominam tenero continuisse sinu
> aut, gelidas hibernus aquas cum fuderit Auster
>   securum somnos imbre iuuante sequi.   (1.1.44-8)

('How pleasant it is to hear the winds rage as I lie here and hold my mistress in my gentle embrace: or else, when the wintry South wind pours out icy showers, to chase sleep without any cares, with the rain sending me to sleep.')

These last lines put the Lucretian passage into the more familiar setting of the Epicurean choosing the life of quiet pleasure rather than that of noise and fame or ruin. The choice is open to all to be either a risk-taking politician or a quietist – but it is a typical stance of the poet to choose the latter in the increasingly common 'choice of life' poems, which seek to justify the choice of apolitical poetry rather than pursue the life of politician, soldier or merchant. Parallels abound in Roman literature: from the first poem in Horace's *Odes* to the explicitly autobiographical account by Ovid of his early life (*Tristia* 4.10.17-40) where the familiar dichotomy of politics and poetry is expressed in peculiarly Roman terms. Virgil also expresses the concept (*Georgics* 4. 563-5), when he describes himself in the closing *sphragis* as:

> illo Vergilium me tempore dulcis alebat
> Parthenope studiis florentem ignobilis otii,
> carmina qui lusi pastorum.

recalling his earlier (*Georgics* 2.486) wish *flumina amem siluasque inglorius* but adding the two important ideas of *otium* and *lusus*. In other words, it may be that if Lucretius appears to be revelling in others' misfortune, he is only doing so to justify his own choice of life as a 'quietist' poet and philosopher. The traditional opposition between poetry and philosophy here gives way to a dichotomy between politics on the one hand and poetry/philosophy on the other, with the philosophical poet espousing a stance which combines the 'childlike' unpolitical nature of a Socrates being taunted by a Callicles and the *otiosus* attitude of a Roman gentleman of letters. Put like this, the *Schadenfreude* of Lucretius becomes a sort of inverted *makarismos* ('happy is he who...') elevating the chosen way of life by invidious contrast with other possibilities. This particular *topos* finds examples throughout classical literature (e.g. Virgil, *Georgics* 2. 458-74; Claudian, *Carminum Minorum Corpusculum* 20; the genre is mocked in Horace, *Epode* 2. More references given in Nisbet and Hubbard [1970] 177), particularly elevating pastoral contentment against the noise of the city, but this is the only example I know of where the favoured 'profession' consists simply in the watching of the others all going wrong.

There is thus more to the present passage than a mere *makarismos*, inverted or not; some positive pleasure is being assigned to the contemplation of the lack of real pleasure suffered by others, rather than just using their displeasure as evidence of the poet's superiority. The *Schadenfreude* of the opening lines gives way, as we saw, to a disquisition on the true nature of pleasure as being the removal of pain and the avoidance of luxury; and the poet ties the two together by asserting that pleasure is simply:

> corpore seiunctus dolor absit, mensque fruatur
> iucundo sensu cura semota metuque   (2.18-19)

which allows for the aesthetic pleasure of watching other men suffer as being literally the enjoyment of a pleasant sensation freed from care and fear.

1   The verb *est* is understood. Most of the line paints a vivid seascape of towering sea (*mari magno*) with the flat surface of the waters (*aequora*) being disturbed by the winds, the ablative phrase *turbantibus aequora uentis* being ablative of attendant circumstances. The reader of the line expects the poet to be imagining the experience of being at sea in a storm – an expectation which the next line will foil. Notice here the parody of epic language: Lucretius is going to build up the scene and then dismiss it.

2   *terra* picks up *mari*, *magnum* picks up *magno*: and it is somebody else (*alterius*) who is suffering (*laborem* here meaning both 'toil' and 'suffering'). The pleasure is all in the watching from the safety of the poet's vantage point.

3-4   Not that it is pleasant/good that others suffer, but because our awareness of our own lack of pain is a pleasure. This has given rise to a lot of discussion, but the essential meaning is as follows:

> pleasure is the greatest good and is to be pursued.
> Pleasure is the removal of want and pain rather than any positive indulgence.
> Therefore the state of contentment which is free from perceived pain is going to be pleasant.

Note how line 4 ends with *suaue* as line 1 began with it, and how *cernere* echoes *spectare* from line 2. The reader is brought into the experience with the second-person verb *careas*, followed by *tui* in the next sentence and then *queas* in line 9.

5-6   After the storm at sea, the battle-scene: made parallel by the repetition of *suaue* and *magna* from line 1 and the variant *tueri* (for *spectare* and *cernere*). *tueri* also has resonance here as the adjective *tutus* ('safe') derives from it ('watched over') and so the poet notes the irony of our safely watching a battle which is *tutus* ('watched') but hardly *tutus* ('safe') – at least for the combatants. The word *campos* ('plains') may remind the Roman reader of the *campus Martius*. The scansion of line 6 makes it clear that *tua* is ablative agreeing with *parte*, the phrase meaning 'without you having any share in the danger'. The 'you' in question (like the second-person verbs at lines 36 and 41) is the 'Ideal Second Person' (i.e. the reader) rather than Memmius.

7-15   After the first two items of spectator pleasure, the poet goes on to the 'greatest pleasure of all' (literally, 'nothing is sweeter than...'). The passage is charged with the sort of political catchwords current in Rome at the time which Lucretius quotes sardonically, as pointed out by Fowler (1989, 134-5): terms such as *labor, niti, rerum potiri* are part of the language of political competition and the contrast between *ingenio* and *nobilitate* indicates a gulf in the Roman class system which excluded most citizens from high office (see 11n.) The whole passage is sardonic as their struggle is for something which will not give them happiness (*opes*) or for something which they have anyway (*rerum*) and it is *sapientia* and not power which will save them. For the contempt for futile struggling cf. 3. 62-93.

7-8   *bene* goes with *munita* ('well fortified'): *templa* is qualified by this phrase and also by *serena* and *edita*: the phrase *doctrina sapientum* goes after *munita* ('fortified by the teaching of the wise'). *edita* lends the sense of 'lofty', while *serena* grants the wise man's abode the contentment

9   (*ataraxia*) which Epicurus said was the goal of philosophy.

9   The wise man is raised on high physically and so naturally can *despicere* ('look down on') those beneath him – a notion reminiscent of Plato, *Sophistes* 216c. *passim* is to be taken with the next line rather than with *uidere*.

10   The people down below are lost (*errare...palantis*) and looking for the way. The phrase *uiam uitae* suggests the metaphorical 'road of life' afforded by philosophy.

11   Two sorts of ambition are here mentioned with parallel verbs *certare... contendere*: 'ability' (*ingenio*) suggests the mark of the *nouus homo*, while *nobilitate* can only connote political eminence in Republican Rome. The term *nobilis* referred to one who had had a consul in the family and was a jealously guarded mark of a surpisingly small number of aristocratic families in Rome of the time – the few who broke into the charmed circle being known as 'new men' (*noui homines*) (cf. Cicero, *Sest.* 136: Syme 10-27).

12   The poet exaggerates for satirical effect: people 'strive' with 'excessive toil' 'night and day' to reach the success they crave. *labore* reminds us of *laborem* in line 2, while *niti* continues the theme of 'striving' after *certare...contendere* in the previous line. The tireless politician who 'never sleeps' (cf. Cicero, *ad Fam.* 9.24.4) has his rhetoric thrown back at him as a sign of his folly.

13   What they are seeking is wealth and property: *opes rerumque* are well juxtaposed as the objects of desire. There may be an implicit reference in *emergere* to the story of Odysseus emerging from the waves (cf. Homer, *Odyssey* 5.388-9), and yet the use of *rerum* is philosophically charged, in a poem *de rerum natura* which explains how we have *res* all around us which we can enjoy freely.

14   The poet apostrophises errant humanity (cf. 5.1194) with accusatives of exclamation. *miser* elsewhere denotes the wretched state of being in an unsuccessful love-affair (4.1076, Catullus 8) and here has the sense of one hankering for what is not available. *caeca* is interesting: after a sequence of five verbs of seeing (*spectare, cernere, tueri, despicere, uidere*) the poet draws the conclusion that people must be blind to persist in their foolish ways, and continues the emphasis on sight with *uidere* in line 16.

15-16 For the image of darkness as philosophical unenlightenment and reason as shedding light, cf. 1.144-5, 3.87-90. *periclis* reminds us of line 6: only the wise man who looks safely on (but does not share in) the *pericla* of others is safe. *hoc aeui quodcumquest* means 'whatever life there is', *quodcumque* acting as a diminutive, as in Catullus 1.8.

16-19 There is no finite verb here but a series of infinitives of exclamation: 'to see that nature barks for nothing else but this, to have pain kept apart from the body and for the mind to enjoy pleasant sensation, freed from anxiety and fear'. (This is to read Marullus' *mensque* for the MS reading *mente*.)

17 The metaphor of *latrare* is that of a dog barking, a metaphor for 'crying out for' going back to Homer (*Odyssey* 20.13) and Ennius (*Annales* 584) and having philosophical edge in reminding the reader of the Cynic school – whose name derived from the Greek word for 'dog' and who preached a similarly reductive style of life.

18 The essential ingredient for happiness is freedom from pain: while some pain will be inevitable and Epicurus died in agony (of 'urine retention and dysentery'), he did not lose his equanimity by remembering past happiness (Diogenes Laertius 10.22). Note here also the correspondence between physical (*corpore*) and mental (*mente*) needs.

19 'Pleasant sensation' is then elaborated as 'free from anxiety and fear', *semota* agreeing with *natura* (understood). As often, pleasure is defined in (to us) negative terms as the absence of pain, both physical and the mental pain of fear. This is partly due to the Epicurean view that pleasure consists in the removal of want in, for example, the ingestion of food or the ejaculation of sperm; partly in the associated austere notion that 'a little is enough' (*paruum quod satis est*) which the poet is going to elaborate in lines 20-36. Once the pain of want has been removed, Epicurus argues, pleasure cannot be increased but only varied (see Epicurus, *Letter to Menoeceus* 130-1).

20 The emphasis on seeing is continued in *uidemus*.

21 The construction of *opus esse* here means simply 'is necessary'. The whole sentence then runs: 'therefore we see that few things are absolutely necessary for our bodily nature'. The subjunctive in *demant* is generic, 'such as may remove pain', and *quae* is separated by tmesis from the *cumque* with which it goes.

22 The sense is clear even if the phrasing is unfamiliar: *uti* introduces the subjunctive *possint* '(we see that we need only such things) as might be able to...' (see OLD s.v. 'ut' 34b). *deliciae* is a term of positive pleasure after the negative terms of line 21: 'delight' rather than simply 'freedom from pain', and delights in large numbers. The metaphor in *substernere* is of 'laying out a bed of luxury' (West [1969] 85): the nature of this natural luxury will become clear in 29-33.

23-33 We have to understand 'anything' with *gratius* ('nor does nature require occasional relief by something more pleasing – even if there are no golden statues of young men...when (*cum*) stretched out on the soft grass...'). The sentence sets up a strong contrast between the false and superficial pleasures of luxuries (gold) and the real available pleasure of lying in the grass by the river.

23   Lucretius personifies *natura* herself as meaning 'human nature'; for this sort of personification, cf. 3.931-63.

24-33   The description of the luxurious palace with its golden statues holding blazing torches, and diners eating while the lyre played and the room gleamed with gold, is unmistakably taken from the description of the proverbially happy and prosperous palace of King Alcinous in Homer, *Odyssey* 7.100-102 (cf. Gale [1994] 106, 111-12). This sets up a neat literary irony as the epic poet Lucretius echoes the father of epic poetry but in terms which he will dismiss as philosophy and thus provides a nice example of Lucretius writing 'the epic to end all epics'.

24   The word *simulacra* is well chosen: at face value it simply means 'statues' but in Epicurean philosophy it connotes the superfine film-like images which are constantly peeling off things and which cause us to perceive the objects and people from which they emanate (see 4. 26-268 for a full explanation of this). These 'films' are as fine and insubstantial as anything can be, and so the word here shows us Lucretius' philosophical purpose: we see 'solid gold' but of course we only *see* 'images' and there is (almost) nothing to them.

25   The Greek word *lampadas* is in the accusative as the object of *retinentia* ('holding torches in their right hands'). Note the neat compound adjective *igniferas*.

26   Notice the oxymoronic juxtaposition of *lumina nocturnis*: the setting is a feast (*epulis*) but Lucretius only mentions this now so as to lead naturally onto the gleaming room and the playing of the lyre.

27-8   Precious metal abounds : *argento...auroque...aurataque*, and the reflection is enhanced by the pair of parallel 'shining' verbs *fulget* (here scanned as two long syllables) and *renidet*, and the 'auditory reflection' of the echo in *reboant. citharae* is dative (the rooms echo to the sound of the lyre) as the echoes appear to make the walls themselves create music (see 4. 572-94). Note also the double adjectival description *laqueata aurata*: the panelled ceiling was mentioned as a symbol of luxury later by Horace (*Odes* 2.16.11, on which see Nisbet and Hubbard [1978] 260). *templa* here means 'rafters' and recalls the same word (used in a different sense) in line 8.

29-30   The luxurious word-painting of lines 27-8 gives way to pastoral idealism:

note the relaxation (*prostrati*) in the 'soft' grass in friendly company (*inter se*). The rafters of the gilded ceiling give way to the branches of the tree, whose size (*altae*) affords good shelter; the music of the lyre gives way to the noise of the running water (which will also provide drink).

31-2   The fools of line 13 strove for *opes* – the wise man does not need great *opes* either to enjoy himself (*iucunde*) or to look after his bodily needs. The poet continues the idyllic scene with smiling weather; for the metaphor, cf. 1.1005, 2.502 (bright peacocks), 4.1125 (fancy slippers); Ennius frag. 457-8.

33   The seasons sprinkle the grass with flowers: note the variation of *herbas* after *gramine* and the verbal placing of the flowers amid the grass in *uiridantis floribus herbas*.

34-6   Fevers are not cured more quickly if the patient is in a luxurious bed. The fever is described as 'hot' (*calidae*) with effective 'c' alliteration and the opulent bed is well depicted in rich language ('woven pictures', 'blushing purple'), while the simple plebeian blanket is shown in two words. The adjective *rubenti* is apt for the bed of a fever-patient; and the terms are unevenly matched in the use of *iacteris* for the rich man 'tossing and turning', while the poor patient simply 'has to lie down'. Once again, the poet sets up a strong contrast between the life of discontented luxury on the one hand and contented poverty – the 'little that is enough' – on the other.

37-9   Luxury is no help to the body, and neither does it help the mind. Note the ordered structure of the sentence: *nil proficiunt...nil prodesse*, the triad of *nil...neque...nec*, the contrast of *corpore* and *animo*.

37   The word *gazae* is pejorative here, evoking the conspicuous consumption of an eastern potentate (see OLD s.v. 'gaza').

38   *nobilitas* recalls line 11 while *gloria regni* is more appropriate to the autocratic rule of the eastern kings. Rome expelled the last of the kings (Tarquin the Proud) in 510 BC and the word *regni* was therefore no longer current, although it became a word of reproach to one's political enemies. The word here carries the strong sense of 'excessive' or 'illicit' power and thus loads the issue firmly towards the apolitical Epicurean stance.

40-6   The sight of troops engaged in military drills might be worthwhile if it scared away your fears.

40   *campi* probably refers to the *Campus Martius* where such drills could be practised. The word *tuas* suggests that the addressee is the sort of person who might command legions.

41   *feruere* is a good metaphor – 'boiling' – used to depict the excitement of physical activity, the frenetic movement of men and also the passionate feelings which such drills arouse: this is of course sardonic here in a context of mere playing at war (for the sense of *simulacra* see above 24n). The word also reminds us of the fever of the sick man in lines 34-6. The addressee reader is, as at the start of the passage, merely looking on the conflict (*uideas*).

42-3 The language becomes epic in style to depict the epic spectacle of military might. *equum ui* recalls Ennius (*Annales* 161, 412), *certamina belli* is a common enough cliché (see OLD s.v. 'certamen' 2b), the serried ranks are well evoked with the repeated *pariter pariterque*, the men equipped both with *armis* and *animis*. Hints of parody show through this epic façade, however: the arms are mere decoration (*ornatas*), as this is only a training exercise; and we only see the 'images' (*simulacra*) anyway, so that we are seeing an image of a mock battle. Little wonder that the fears are not themselves frightened by it.

44-5 The fears refuse to flee: notice the repetition of *timefactae...pauidae... timores*. If your legions playing at war could rout *these* enemies (the poet is saying) then there would be some point to it. Note also the alliteration of 't' and 'r'. *religio* is once again the monstrous enemy (cf. 1.62-4) to be defeated; *animo* means 'from your mind'. There is irony in the notion that 'fears of death' – a normal emotion felt in time of war (e.g. Homer, *Iliad* 9. 1-3) – might flee in terror, the fear being itself frightened. The irony only serves to accentuate the folly of such an idea.

46 The true Epicurean ideal of mental *ataraxia*: the 'emptiness' contained in *uacuum* means 'empty of fears'.

47-54 The military drills are now seen as farce; for the use of *ludibrio*, cf. Livy 37.41.12 where the pretend battle is abandoned in favour of a real one – *amoto inani ludibrio*. The strutting soldiers are themselves two-dimensional (*simulacra*) figures of fun (*ridicula*), while the fears themselves walk tall among the grandees of this world (*reges rerumque potentes*) and have no respect at all for the appearances of wealth and power which they display (52).

48-9 Fears are not themselves afraid of anybody – a nice psychological touch of realism and an interesting paradox. *sequaces* evokes the sense of anxiety 'dogging' the steps of the worried man wherever he goes. *fera* is sarcastic, as these weapons are not 'savage' enough to frighten the enemy fear.

50 *rerumque potentes* picks up line 13 and is similarly sardonic: the men of power only have an empty show of authority over *res* when (again) real *res* are all around us for the taking.

51   The theme of worthless wealth is picked up: the 'gleaming' and the 'gold' are like those of the palatial dinner of 24-8, while the rich purple of the clothing is like the useless purple blanket covering the sick man in 34-6. *fulgorem* is repeated in *splendorem*, while the colour gold is matched by the colour crimson. *purpura* refers to the dye collected from the *murex* shellfish of a deep crimson colour.

53   Wealth and 'power' cannot move fear: this is the real power of *ratio*. Note how earlier Epicurus' victory over religion was told in terms of an epic contest (1.62-79) and how later on his ridding the world of fear is compared favourably with Hercules' ridding the world of monsters (5.22-54). This line is unusual for suppressing final 's' in two words (*omnis...rationis*).

54   *omnis* is picked up from the previous line. The image of life being a struggle in the dark is effective.

55-61 These lines occur three times (cf. 3.87-93, 6.35-41); this sort of repetition is one of the features which has led some to believe that Lucretius did not live to complete his poem, but it is also arguable that such repetition is 'Homeric' (Homer repeats whole passages) and may also be useful for the didactic tone of his work. Note the variation of vocabulary as Lucretius finds different ways to express 'fear' (*trepidant, metuunt, timemus, metuenda, pauitant, terrorem*) and the strong contrast of light and darkness.

55   The comparison of the unenlightened with children is used by Plato (*Phaedo* 77e; contrast Callicles calling philosophy itself 'childish' in Plato, *Gorgias* 485a4-d2 and see Gale [1994] 49). *caecis* means both 'blind' (cf. 14) and also 'unseen': even when we are in daylight our minds are still in the dark.

56   The parallel is verbally drawn between *in tenebris metuunt* and *in luce timemus*.

57   The sentence runs: *quae sunt nilo magis metuenda quam* ('which are no more to be feared than...').

58   *finguntque futura* is a neat depiction of the imagined terrors about to occur with harsh alliteration of letter 'f'.

59-61 A *leitmotif* of the poem is that only philosophy can dispel these fears and this passage is repeated here from 1.146-8. *animi* can be taken with both *terrorem* and *tenebras*, which are in effect the same thing.

60   There is a clear jingle here between the *radii* and the *ratio*. Note also how the 'weapons' of daylight will not scatter the darkness, an epic phrase reminding us both of the need for the heroic endeavour of Epicurus (cf. 53n above) and also of the epic tradition in which the poem is composed.

61 *species* is what we can see – the natural phenomena of the world – while *ratio* is the atomic system itself which explains these phenomena, the 'workings' of Nature.

After this ethical introduction, the poet goes on to describe the movement of atoms: one problem for the ancient atomist was to explain how, if all things fall downwards with gravity and if atoms are all in perpetual freefall through space, they ever manage to form compounds at all. Atoms (critics would say) are all falling like raindrops in parallel lines through space. The 'answer' to this is the famous theory of the *clinamen* or 'swerve'; it asserts that atoms swerve from the straight downward path and thus set up a ricochet-effect which makes other atoms bounce against each other and form units of matter out of which things as we see them are formed (62-332).

The poet next discusses variety of atomic shapes: he has already shown that space and matter are infinite (1.921-1051). There is no reason why the atoms could not be identical in form except that the variety of phenomena lends credence to the notion of a variety in atomic shape. This proposition is examined in lines 333-70, where the poet proves that atomic variety is huge by showing how animals recognise their own young, in a passage of great emotional power and poetic beauty.

333 The main verb in the sentence is the imperative *percipe* in line 335, with the series of indirect questions attached to it. *exordia rerum* means literally 'the starting-points of things' and here stands for simply 'atoms' (*primordia*).

335 *multigenis* is only found in this passage: note the variation of *formis... figuris* and *longe distantia...uariata*.

336-7 'Not that there are insufficient numbers of them endowed with similar shape but because they are generally not all equal to all others.' Lucretius is arguing that there will be an infinite number of atoms of a finite number of shapes. Note the polyptoton of *omnibus omnia* and the variation of *sint...constant*.

338-9 Lucretius has shown that the number of atoms is infinite just as space is infinite. If the range of atomic variety were also infinite, then there would have to be atoms of visible size – even atoms of infinite size – and as this is obviously not the case then the range of variety must be finite. *copia* here means 'number'; *neque finis...neque summa* is something of a tautology but with a different emphasis, *finis* referring to the 'end' of the labour of counting them, *summa* referring to the total number to be recorded.

340-1   The same idea as at lines 336-7, but now embellished with the metaphor of *filo* (literally 'thread', here 'texture').

342-8   Moving from microscopic atomic matter to the visible world, Lucretius shows how there is a vast array of different types of living thing and that even within the species there is a further array of variety of life-form. Humans, fish, cattle, wild beasts are all listed briefly in two lines; better evidence is afforded by birds and so Lucretius devotes three lines to them alone. The passage is more than a catalogue of variety: note how the poet conveys energetic activity by showing these life-forms moving and living, rather than mounted and stuffed.

342   The human race is a good example of superficially similar forms which are, however, all distinct; but Lucretius does not dwell on this, listing humans as simply a *genus* distinct from that of fish. The fish are elegantly and economically described as 'mute swimmers of the scaly kind', with *squamigerum* a genitive plural of the adjective *squamiger* used as a noun.

343   *laeta* here means 'sleek' rather than 'happy', but the sense of joy is also present – as in *laetantia* in the next line.

344-6   Lucretius looks at birds of water and woodland: their numbers are brought out in the verbs *concelebrant* ('throng') and *peruolgant* ('crowd') and also in the range of habitat specified (river-bank, springs, lakes, woodland). The poet's aesthetic pleasure in the birds shows in the adjectives *laetantia* ('joyful' transferred from the observer to the observed) and *auia* ('pathless' – almost 'far from the madding crowd'; cf. 1.926).

347-8   After the long list of animals and birds of various haunts, the poet challenges us to take 'any one of them' and see how they are different even within the species, his confidence made clear in the certain second-person singular future indicative (*inuenies*).

349-51   Otherwise the mother and the young would not know each other; this is leading on to the famous description which follows of the calf separated from its mother. Note the repetition of *proles matrem...mater prolem*) showing the reciprocity of the recognition. The argument is advanced by the repetition also of *posset...posse*; 'no less than (*atque*) humans' prepares for the pathetic and emotional description which is to follow.

352-66   The tale of the cow looking in anguish for her calf, which has been taken away and sacrificed, goes far beyond the requirements of this argument in range of detail; it manages also to attack the superstitious belief which causes this innocent animal's suffering – thus killing two birds with the same Epicurean stone. For Lucretius' mockery of sacrifice as a means to an end, cf. 4.1233-9.

352   *saepe* shows that Lucretius is not here finding some isolated example but a common instance to prove a general point. *deum* is genitive plural for *deorum*: there is sardonic tone in *decora* of the shrines of the gods which 'looked wonderful'.

353 *turicremas* is both scenic detail and a jibe at the odd ritual employed. *mactatus concidit* go together in effective juxtaposition ('falls down slaughtered').

354 This line adds nothing to the atomic argument being advanced but is highly expressive of the pathos of the situation and the cruelty of the ritual. Note the hyperbole of 'a hot river of blood' and the gruesome detail of *exspirans* to show that the blood came like breath out of the calf's mouth.

355 The cow is endowed with all the feelings of a human mother; and her loss is that of a woman who has lost a child (*orbata*). The detail of how she 'wanders through the green glades' recalls lines 344-6, but replaces the happy thronging of nature with wretched misery.

356 The final word of the line is the only 'bovine' feature here: the pathetic detail of *bisulcis* shows us the cow ignoring all prints which are not 'cloven'. There is a form of dramatic irony in this description as we the readers know that the search for the calf is a waste of time.

357 *si queat* here means 'to see if she might be able to...'. *oculis* is perhaps redundant after *conuisens* but the phrase emphasises the frantic searching of the mother-cow.

358 To the mother-cow she has lost a *fetus* ('offspring') with which she has been pregnant; and she now 'fills' the grove with lamentation.

359 The compound adjective *frondiferum* well evokes the scene of a leafy grove, while *adsistens* is brilliant in giving us a picture of the cow – which has been wandering frantically – suddenly standing still to utter her desperate cries. *crebra* here means 'frequently', the adjective being used as a adverb.

360 In fact it was the calf which was literally *perfixa* when it was sacrificed, but the mother-cow is 'pierced with longing' just as painfully.

361-3 Nothing will delight the mother-cow or remove her sense of loss. The delights of nature are listed with telling adjectives: 'tender' willows, grass 'thriving with dew', rivers gliding along at the top of the banks (i.e. full to the brim). What she wants is the tender calf, not tender willows; she wants the calf to be 'thriving' and not the grass; the rivers cannot please her, just as no other calf can *deriuare* her cares in line 365. That the anxiety is *subitam* is another fine example of Lucretius' ability to understand the world he describes, as the cow never worried in the past about losing a calf until now – and now the loss is total.

364-5 To us, perhaps, all calves look alike, and the mother-cow will have found many another calf in her travels; but none of them could take the place of the one she has lost, and she knows her own by its *species. laeta* is bitterly ironic as no grass can be 'happy' now.

367-70 After the high pathos of lines 352-66, the poet turns to more cheerful examples of the same phenomenon. Note the detail of the 'quavering voices' of the kids, the 'horned mothers', 'butting' lambs and 'bleating flocks', rounded off with the entertaining *fere* – all proving a generalised statement. Lucretius, as often, does not merely state a rule: he animates it into a film of real life (complete with sound-effects) which we recognise, and convinces us as much by the quality of his description as by the logic of his argumentation.

370 *fere* shows Lucretius' powers of observation at their best: lambs and kids do occasionally go to the wrong udder, and so their ability to run to 'their own' milk is not infallible.

Book Three

'Death is nothing to us'

This passage forms part of the great diatribe against the fear of death with which the third book – and the first half of the poem – ends. The 'moral' purpose of the poem is to liberate man from fear of the gods and from fear of death, and this rests on the demonstration that:

> we are made up of matter
> matter disintegrates into its component parts
> therefore we too will not exist after we have died.

There is no room in the materialist universe for disembodied spirits, and so we need not fear anything after death because there will not *be* anything after death. The passage shows Lucretius at his finest: sardonic and sarcastic in his mockery of the mourners or the maudlin dinner-guest, angry when speaking with the voice of Nature who points out that we have enjoyed our lives and must now make way for others to do the same, incisive and imaginative in his allegorisation of the fabled torments meted out to the sinners, logical and emotional at the same time.

830 The phrase is a direct translation of the words of Epicurus himself (*Kyriai Doxai* 2,71: Cicero, *de finibus* 2.100). *nec...hilum* is a strong negative ('not a bit').

831 *mors* is nothing since the soul is proved to be *mortalis*; and yet (one might respond) the reaction to death would in fact be a great deal less hysterical if the soul were <u>not</u> *mortalis*.

832   *nil aegri* goes together ('nothing of suffering', i.e. 'no suffering').

833   The Punic Wars were – like the Persian Wars to the ancient Athenian – seen as the turning point in Roman history, the razor's edge of fate, and Lucretius playfully builds up the epic imagery to suit the importance of the conflict and also to act as a foil to the simple truth that to the unborn (and the dead) all this is of no significance. Note here the pomposity of the spondaic gerund *confligendum* and the faint hyperbole of *undique* ('attacking from all directions').

834   The hyperbole continues as 'all things' were 'shaken' and 'quaked' at the war. *tumultu/ horrida contremuere* is probably (as Bailey notes) an imitation of Ennius, *Annales* 310: *Africa terribili tremit horrida terra tumultu*; and the whole sentence emphasises the shaking and trembling of war (*trepido...horrida contremuere*).

835   The second half of the line may seem redundant (Kenney glosses it as 'on earth') but it has the effect of showing that the conflict was high as well as wide: if 'everywhere' shook with war, then the skies must have been ringing with the noise.

836-7   For a while it was uncertain who would rule the world. This is again somewhat hyperbolic, but was the view taken by Livy (29.17.6: 'what is being fought for now is the question of whether the human race should regard you or the Carthaginians as the rulers of the earth'). Line 837 is exaggerated: not only 'all humanity' but 'by land and sea' as well. The phrase is added to look forward to line 842.

838-40   Lucretius' language appears very didactic at this point: he is anxious to remind us that:

        a) we are formed of body and soul
        b) body and soul split up at death
        c) therefore 'we' will not exist after death

and he conveys these three points in reverse order. The sense of 'splitting' in *corporis atque animai/ discidium* ('splitting') is itself split over the line in enjambement.

840   It would clearly be self-contradictory to deny the phrasing here: if we do not exist, then by definition nothing can happen to 'us'.

841   *sensus* is the ability to feel and this is produced by the *anima* atoms spread throughout the body. Earlier in the book Lucretius has explained the mechanics of this by reference to such things as our feeling – or not feeling – a tiny insect walking on our hand (381-95).

842   The argument is *a fortiori*: if we cannot feel the earth and the sea being

mixed together, then we will (all the more) be unable to feel smaller things happen to us. The reference to the mixing of earth and sea, sea and sky, is picked up from the description of the Punic wars and rounds off the section neatly.

843-6 The argument is as follows: even if the soul atoms could feel anything, that would not affect us as we need both body and soul to be persons capable of feeling anything. Lucretius uses this argument partly because he has already proven that the individual atoms are eternal; and so if he has also proved that soul-atoms feel sensation, then he might have to admit that the soul could continue to feel after the death of the body. He answers this with the decisive assertion that 'we' are made up of body and soul and that if the union be dissolved (as it obviously is at death) then 'we' cease to exist.

845 *nil ad nos* repeats 830, just as the following phrase reminds us of line 839.

847-51 In an atomic universe where the atoms themselves are eternal, it is perfectly possible for the same combinations of atoms to recur: and so the atomic *concilium* which is a human being might thus reassemble and 'recreate' the same body. This would seem to offer at least a statistical possibility of life after death; but Lucretius denies that we would be the same person as the awareness of ourselves (*repetentia nostri*) would have been broken by death and so it would in effect be a new person made of the old atoms.

The long sentence is held together by the string of parallel verbs (*collegerit...redegerit...fuerint*) and especially by the use of *nostram... nobis...nos...nostri*, whereby he can argue that although 'we' are reassembled, it will not be of any import (*pertineat*) to 'us' – a paradox which only the final line explains.

848-9 The atoms are reconstituted in the same place and a fresh allocation of life/time is given to us: note the difference between *rursus* (from *reuersus* and having a spatial sense of 'back to where it started') and *iterum* with a temporal sense of 'all over again'. The 'light of life' is a common poetic phrase: cf. 1.22-3.

852-61 Lucretius, as often, proves his thinking with the familiar line of argument:

if P, then Q
but not-Q
therefore not-P

In this case the reasoning is: if we are to be the same person we will remember our previous lives; but we have no memory of previous lives, therefore we shall not be the same person.

852	*ad nos de nobis* is deliberately paradoxical: *nos* is our present personality, while *nobis* is the former life; both may count as 'us' but the argument makes it clear that they are not in fact the same person. The poet is thus making the philosophical point in verbal form.
853	*angor* is a surprising touch: all that the context requires is for the poet to show that no recollection links the old self to the present one, but he cannot resist adding the sardonic comment that grief for our dead selves does not touch us even if we are reconstituted again, and so there is no possibility of suffering after death.
854-5	Note the expansive phrasing of *immensi temporis omne/ praeteritum spatium*, expressive in verbal form of the vast expanse of time, here seen in spatial terms (*respicias...spatium*).
855-6	The movement of atoms has been described and explained in Book 2: the atoms are constantly moving and forming new combinations that make up the physical world we experience, and of which we are a part.
857	*semina* is a common Lucretian word for 'atoms'. The poet now asserts that this statistical possibility in fact has happened 'often'.
858	Note the contrast of *nunc sumus* and *ante fuisse*.
859	*memori* goes with *mente* ('with a remembering mind').
860	The tmesis of *inter enim iectast* (for *interiectast enim*) is an obvious verbal ploy to depict the 'break in life' in verbal form. For another instance of this word-painting see 5.287 where the sun's light is broken verbally in *radios inter quasi rumpere lucis*.
861	'All the atomic motions have wandered off all over from those sensations.' Sensation is the result of atomic movement – so even if the atoms are the same their movements are not and so sensation is now different. Note the theme of 'wandering' contained in *uage...deerrarunt* and the appropriate way in which 'movements' (*motus*) are wandering all over the place.
862-9	After the parenthetic explanation that even eternal atoms cannot render 'us' alive again, Lucretius now returns to his main theme. To suffer requires a sufferer, and after death it will be as if we had never been born. Therefore there can be no suffering after death. The purpose of this passage – and one major purpose of the whole poem – is to take away the fear of suffering after death, and so the poet removes that possibility. He does not contemplate the possibility that life after death might be pleasant.
862	The construction of *esse* + adverb is common enough in Latin (OLD s.v. 'sum' 13b) and here means 'if one is to be wretched and sick...'. The construction of the sentence is: *debet...ipse esse...cui* – 'the man to

whom bad is to happen must exist himself at that time'.

864   *probet* is a shortened form of *prohibet*.

865   *conciliari* is an excellent word to choose as it suggests the atomic compounds (*concilia*) which form all things, and so as the old *concilia* have scattered, there can be no *conciliari* of suffering.

866-8   The infinitives depend on *scire licet* ('we may be sure that').

867   'he who does not exist cannot be made wretched'.

868   Not only is he no longer alive, it is as if he had never been alive at all. Note the word *natus* placed at the end of one line followed by *mortalem* at the start of the next.

869   The idea that death cannot itself die is an old one and well brought out here by the repetition of *mortalem...mors...immortalis*, with our short life (*uitam*) encased in words of death.

870-93   The fate of the body after death is of no importance to us. Lucretius passes from reasoned argument to mockery of the empty fears of people.

870   *proinde* means 'accordingly' and shows that Lucretius regards the next point as being derived from his proof that the dead can feel nothing. *uideas* is the second-person subjunctive addressed to the reader.

871-2   Three fates are singled out – burial, cremation or being eaten by animals. The third would presumably be most likely to happen to those who die in battle. Note the shortened form *posto* for *composito*. *interfiat* is the passive form of *interficere* and as such is deliberately misleading here: the poet is arguing that the fate of the corpse is immaterial to the dead man, yet he puts a word into the dying man's mouth which suggests that the man is thinking of being <u>killed</u> by burning. The whole point of the passage is thus focussed, as it is precisely this confusion between the feelings of the living and the lack of them in the dead which the poet is seeking to dispel. The reference to 'the jaws of beasts' may suggest the plot of Sophocles' *Antigone* where the eponymous heroine dies rather than see her dead brother become carrion of this kind.

873   The metaphor in *sincerum* is that of a pot being tested for flaws: cf. Horace, *Epistles* 1.2.54 for the word used of a perfect pot. The line has a notable amount of 's' alliteration.

874   A *stimulus* was a goad used for stirring a reluctant animal into action: cf. 4.1082-3. *caecus* here means 'unseen' (as at Virgil, *Aeneid* 4.2) but also has the sense of 'blind', as the theme of the unenlightened being blind to the truth is never far away in Lucretius (e.g. 2.14). The phrase is interesting here: Lucretius is referring to the man who claims to believe that death is the end of bodily sensation and yet fears the fate of his corpse. His *stimulus* is his irrational fear which it is the purpose of the poem to illuminate with the light of philosophy.

876 'For (as I believe) he does not grant what he claims and the source [of the claim]': i.e. he does not really believe what he professes (that the dead do not feel anything), and does not really accept the truth behind this belief (that the soul dies when separated from the body at death). Lucretius' phrasing is more lively than this would suggest: not to 'give what one promises' is a common enough accusation of cheating dishonesty in matters financial and also sexual (cf. Catullus 110), just as *unde* often means 'the wherewithal' to pay one's debts (cf. Plautus, *Captiui* 850, Petronius 45.6). The man Lucretius is describing is an intellectual cheat who wants to have the credit for the 'right' opinions but will not surrender his emotional capital.

877 The metaphor becomes more extreme: the man now will not uproot himself and throw himself out, like a tree which must be uprooted fully and not merely cut off at the base. His deep-seated feelings are like the roots of the tree which remain invisibly below the surface even after the rest has been removed.

878 *esse...super* = *superesse*, an example of tmesis. For *facit* meaning 'he pretends' cf. Catullus 97.9. *inscius* neatly concludes the sentence with a reminder that this behaviour is the result of ignorance, the juxtaposition with *ipse* showing that the man is ignorant – of himself.

879 The first word is strongly stressed: and *uiuus* is of course the key to the sentence. While he is alive, the fool cannot imagine his body being hurt without his feeling it. Note the vague term *futurum* at the end of the line – the next line will make this all too specific.

880 For birds and beasts tearing at the dead body compare Catullus 108 with its fantasy of such mauling happening to the poet's enemy, and cf. also Ovid, *Ibis* (derived from a lost poem of Callimachus).

It was a common belief in Greece that bodies which did not receive proper burial would not be able to go down to the underworld (see, for example, Homer, *Iliad* 23.71, Sophocles, *Antigone*); unburied bodies in Rome were thought of as malignant and hungry ghosts, the *lemures*, appeased at the festival of the Lemuria in May.

881 *miseret* is usually an impersonal verb in Latin: here it is used personally with *sui* ('he pities himself'). The man as he is now (*ipse*) is pitying the future 'self' (*sui*).

881-3 Lucretius uses four verbs in these three lines, two negatives (*neque diuidit... nec remouet*) and two positive ones (*fingit...contaminat*). The image of *diuidit* ('separates') is enhanced by the manner in which the verb separates *se* from *illim. remouet* has to understand *se* again ('removes himself'); *proiecto corpore* gives us the picture of the corpse lying 'cast out' and unburied, reminding the reader that this corpse is to be mauled by birds and animals (880). The enjambement of *illum/ se* is highly efffective: the fool thinks that the two are the same, but the poetry shows us the gulf between them; and *astans* creates a picture of the still living man 'standing' by the prostrate corpse – an image repeated in 887. *contaminat* is a powerful verb to use, the poet provocatively suggesting that the fool is thus 'spoiling' a corpse with his own feelings whereas corpses are usually seen as the source and site of corruption rather than its object. The verb thus has the senses of 'dishonour' 'adulterate' and 'violate', neatly using the traditional notion of the uncleanness of the corpse and turning it round into a philosophical point whereby the corpse is clean and it is the living who are the agents of corruption.

884   *hinc* is inferential ('this is why he...'). *indignatur* picks up *indignarier* from line 870.

885   *in uera...morte* means 'in death at it really is'. Notice the three juxtaposed pairs of words to mock the notion of the living-dead person: *alium se... sibi si...stansque iacentem*.

886   The inanity of the idea is stressed by the self-contradiction of a man who is *uiuus* complaining that he is *peremptum.*

887   The image in *stansque iacentem* is that of a ghost standing over his own dead body. The rhythm is also unusual – Roman poets avoid word-end after the second foot especially when (as here) the first foot is a dactyl as it makes the beginning of the line sound like the end of a line. The strong metrical pause of the false ending is effective in evoking the delusion of the man who thinks his death is likewise a false close (when it is in fact final). The infinitives depend on *dolere* which in turn depends on *possit* ('who could grieve at being torn to pieces...'). *uri* is added to look forward to other forms of disposal as described in the following lines.

888-93   If being eaten by birds and animals is bad, why is it any worse than other means of disposal of the dead? The idea was common in Epicurean thought (cf. Philodemus, *de morte* 32) and in earlier Greek thought: cf. Bion's remarks:

> if you are not buried but thrown out without a tomb, what is bad about that? What is the difference between being burned by fire or eaten by crows on the surface of the earth or being bored into by worms?
>   (cited by Bailey)

The poet here overstates the case deliberately, bringing out the horror of all manner of disposal of the dead: his purpose is to show that none of them is any worse than the others – but the degree of detail is perhaps surprising if his purpose in the book is to reduce our horror of physical death.

888 Note the obvious alliteration of 'm' and the play on *malis malumst* as the poet dwells first on the jaws (*malis*) of the animals and then the act of biting (*morsu*).

889 *tractari* here has the sense of being 'mauled' or 'dragged about' (Bailey), the verb being stressed by being placed in enjambement at the beginning of the line and the end of the phrase. *qui* here means 'how'.

890 The line contains four words to connote heat/fire (*ignibus...calidis torrescere flammis*) in a line of only five words, the participle *impositum* well evoking the placing of the corpse on top of a burning pyre.

891 Honey was used in embalming the corpse (cf. Nepos, *Agesilaus* 8.7), just as it was used for preserving fruit (Columella 12.10.5, Pliny, *Natural History* 15.65). This embalming was only temporary: more permanent embalming procedures are described in vivid detail by Herodotus (2.86-88). Note the strong 's' alliteration and how the instantaneous effect of being *situm* is that the man is *suffocari*. *rigere* is what one expects of the dead, the defining term *frigore* contrasting well with the hot flames of line 890.

892 The body, after being embalmed, is laid out on a cold slab in a rock tomb: this lack of covering contrasts (as Kenney points out) with the state of being buried where one has all too much covering. Note in this line the stress on coldness (*frigore...gelidi*).

893 The paragraph ends with the final fate of being buried under the earth, from lying on top of a cold slab (892) to lying underneath a massive weight of earth.

894-908 Lucretius now puts words into the mouths of imaginary mourners, as later on he makes Nature speak (3. 931-77) and as Plato has the Laws speak at *Crito* 50a (see further 6.1241-2n). This device (known as *prosopopoea*) is used a good deal in satire (Horace, *Epode* 2, *Satires* 2.7, Juvenal 3, for instance), but the first paragraph of the present passage is no cheap *in memoriam* verse thrown together to mock the mourner's bad Latin. There is a neat tricolon crescendo of the house, the wife and then the children, each with their own adjective of approval – the house is *laeta* (a nice use of the pathetic fallacy), the wife is *optima* and the children *dulces* (reinforced by *dulcedine* in the next line), complete with the psychologically telling adjective *tacita* expressing the inner feelings of the father which he keeps to himself; and the vignette of the children fighting for the kiss encapsulates the meeting of the parent and children – with the root *curro* in *occurrent* showing their haste, as does also the prefix *prae* in *praeripere*.

The passage has occasioned a lot of comment, much of it adverse. Lucretius is not trying to persuade the reader to be cavalier about his family's future, nor is he mocking the altruistic urge to provide for one's children. The speech expresses the impotence of the mourners who now see that the dead man will no longer be able to enjoy life in order to emphasise that he will not be suffering at all. From the mourner's point of view things *are* pretty bleak – but the dead man is by now oblivious to all that.

897-8 The anxiety about the future caused by the death of the protector of the family is a common theme in epic; cf. Andromache's anxiety in Homer, *Iliad* 22. 490-507 and Priam's anxiety about his humiliation after death (22. 66-76). The phrase *factis florentibus* is to be taken together as a dative parallel to *tuis*: 'you will not be able to be a *praesidium* to your prosperity and your family'. *misero misere* is a nice use of repetition in the sort of incantatory manner familiar in laments.

898-9 The stakes are high: 'one day' has removed 'all these – so many – prizes of life'. *uitae* is stressed at the end of the sentence and the line: life is itself the thing which has gone and taken so many good things with it.

900-1 After the expressive poetry of lines 894-9, this sentence is prosaic and coldly logical. *earum rerum* presumably refers to the *praemia uitae*. The mourners ought to continue their address to the dead man (*tibi*) in this way – and yet (if the poet is correct) there will be no point in addressing him at all.

902-3 *uideo* is often used of mental understanding; the phrase *dictisque sequantur* is logically unnecessary, as the fear will go whether the mourners speak or not.

904-8 The poet's tone now becomes more directly satirical. The focus of the attack shifts to the unworthy recriminations of the bereaved who seem to envy the corpse who is safely and happily dead (*cunctis priuatu' doloribus aegris* is almost a definition of Epicurean contentment) while they live on to mourn. This both confirms the Epicurean position that death is a state of freedom from all sensation while also parodying the sorrows of the bereaved. The style becomes more inflated with the long words of 907, the pair of compound words *horrifico cinefactum*, the hyperbolic *insatiabiliter* ('whose only other use in Lucretius is of swine rolling in filth, 6.978' (West [1969] 29)). The mourners give the poet an easy target in their self-contradictory argument:

the corpse is safely free of pain
we will all one day die
therefore no grief can be eternal.

904   *aeui quod superest* is to be taken together ' for what is left of time'. Notice the soporific 's' alliteration of *sopitus, sic...superest.*

905   The final letter of *priuatus* has to be elided for the line to scan. This archaic feature (common in Ennius) occurs in Lucretius 49 times. Note also the strong phrase *doloribus aegris.*

907   A line unusual in only containing three words and a single caesura. The tone is one of mockery of the sort of tombstone-verses which mourners wrote.

908   Mockery of the mourners' conceit that they will never stop grieving for the dead man; and also a nice contrast to line 899: one day has robbed him of life, but no day will ever remove their grief.

909-11   The logical answer is tellingly made by the poet: if all things will die, then grief itself will one day die and so eternal grief is impossible (*possit*). However, the poet adds the effective touch of *somnum...atque quietem* to show that this death (which will remove grief) is itself a state of rest and so (implicitly) preferable to 'wasting away in eternal grief' – as well as reminding the mourner of how the dead man is *leto sopitus* (line 904), and so is (by their own admission) not suffering. As often, the poet states the case with emotional as well as analytical force.

910   *res* is vague (cf. 5.1141) but also alludes to the *rerum natura* which the poem is explaining, and which demands that all things (including the earth itself) will one day die.

911   *tabescere* is also used of the effects of love at 4.1120.

912-30   'Eat, drink and be merry...' The poet proceeds to mock the sad and desperate clinging to pleasure which the fear of death induces in the unenlightened. The Roman banquet was the perfect setting for this sort of maudlin talk, as well as being a constant butt of satire throughout Roman literature (Horace, *Satires* 2.8, Juvenal 5, Petronius, *Satyricon*: see Gowers 109-219).

912   *discubuere* reminds us that Roman diners reclined on couches.

913   The importance of the drinking is clear in the prominent position the word *pocula* enjoys. The diners have adorned their brows (*ora*) with garlands, as they often did (cf., for example, Horace, *Odes* 1.38 with Nisbet and Hubbard, Ovid, *Ars Amatoria* 1. 582, OLD s.v. 'corona' 1b).

914-15   The verse spoken by the diners is similar to that produced by Petronius' Trimalchio (*Satyricon* 34):

eheu, nos miseros, quam totus homuncio nil est
sic erimus cuncti postquam nos auferet Orcus
ergo uiuamus dum licet esse bene

('alas for us poor men, how the whole of little man is as nothing. This is how we will be when Orcus will take us away; so let us live while we can enjoy ourselves').

Note here the diminutive *homullis* (from *homo*) and the effective use of the future perfect tense *fuerit* (it will have been: cf. Panthus' words in Virgil, *Aeneid* 2. 325). *post* is adverbial ('afterwards').

916-18 The poet offers a sarcastic explanation of the diners' behaviour: they are behaving as if death were to be a state of thirst and so they are 'filling up' now.

917 The dry thirst is well brought out by the two 'burning' verbs *exurat* and *torrat* and the adjective *arida*.

918 After the vividness of the thirst of line 917, this line is somewhat prosaic and the rhythm of the line is deliberately bumpy; the final word *rei* is scanned as a monosyllable, ending the line with a sense of discord and unevenness.

919-30 The argument is an *a fortiori* syllogism.

> We do not miss our pleasures in sleep
> Death is a much deeper state of unconsciouness than sleep
> therefore *a fortiori* we will not miss our bodily pleasures when we are dead.

For the comparison of death with a dreamless sleep, cf. Socrates in Plato, *Apology* 40c5-e4 and Cicero, *Tusculan Disputations* 1.92.

919 *se uitamque* is surprising as the object of *requirit* ('misses himself and his life') but is well-chosen: the sleeper is unaware of his own existence (*se*) and is also unaware whether he is alive or not – a point which the comparison with the sleep of death will enhance.

921 Once asleep we do not care if we ever wake up again: *per nos* has the sense 'for all we care'.

922 The juxtaposition of *nostri nos* is again effective (cf. 881, 885) to point up the gulf between our conscious selves and our unconscious selves.

923-5 The statement here looks forward to the much fuller discussion of sleep in 4.907-61, where Lucretius explains that in sleep the soul-atoms are scattered, some out of the body and some deep within it, the connection between the soul-atoms which form consciousness being thereby broken until we reassemble them on awaking (see 925). The argument is again syllogistic:

we can awaken quickly from sleep because the soul-atoms cannot
have dispersed far
we cannot awaken from death
therefore the soul-atoms must disperse much further at death.

If perception is the result of the soul-atoms sending messages,
and we have no perception in sleep
then there can be even less perception in death than there is in sleep.

924   *primordia* are the atoms. Lucretius believes that perception is the result of atomic movement of a particular kind and so in sleep the atoms desist from these 'sense-giving movements' (*sensiferis motibus*) and set up different movements of a random nature which do not impinge on our sense-organs, 'wandering' away but ready to be gathered up again at a moment's notice.

925   *correptus* has the sense of 'startled' suddenly.

926-7   If we have no sensation in sleep, then death will present even less sensation – allowing the poet the wry remark that this is true 'if there can be anything less than nothing', with the provocative use of *uidemus* in a context where we will not actually see anything.

926   The phrase *minus ad nos* reminds us of the phrase with which this section began (830, *nil igitur mors est ad nos*) and acts as a form of closure at the end of this section.

928   *turba et disiectus materiai* must mean 'disturbance and dislocation of matter', i.e. the ordered system of *anima* is disturbed and the perceptual links between soul-atoms are broken in sleep and death.

929   *consequitur* is intransitive here, with *leto* meaning 'in death'. Note the repetition of *ex-* in *expergitus exstat*.

930   A suitably epic line to round off the passage. Death is 'cold' as in Greek poetry (cf., for example, Hesiod, *Works and Days* 153, Euripides, frag. 916.6-7) and as also in 3.401 and 3.530 of this poem: the phrase *uitai pausa* ('a break in life') for 'death' draws attention to the fact that unlike sleep (which is enjoyed daily) this particular sort of *pausa* can only be done once (*semel*). *secuta* ('overtaken') is the language of the battlefield where the enemy outstrips us and takes away our life.

931-77   Nature rebukes the man who is reluctant to die. The poet again uses prosopopoiea (see 894-908n) as he has already done in the case of the mourners and the maudlin banqueter. In those instances the device is used to satirise the feelings of the speaker; in this case the purpose is very different. By having Nature upbraid 'one of us' (*alicui nostrum*) Lucretius associates himself with the unenlightened and avoids adopting a lofty tone which would alienate his readers. Later on (1024-52) he puts words into the reader's mouth and again manages to deliver the correct ideas and sentiments without making the reader feel that he is being personally mocked or despised. Horace was to adopt similar tactics in imparting his own advice in the *Satires* (e.g. having his slave berate him in 2.7).

The tone of this passage is varied and keeps our interest. There is gentle reasoning, more aggressive tones then taken towards the old man, logical analysis and aphoristic *sententiae* (e.g. 971), rounded off with rhetorical questions and an image of peace and sleep.

931   It is appropriate that *rerum natura* should speak – as 'she' is after all the subject of the whole poem.

933   Nature uses colloquial Latin to address us. *quid tibi tantopere est?* means 'what is it that bothers you so much that you...'. Her vocative address to *mortalis* is of course highly apt: it is his mortal status which is the thing which is bothering him. For the lofty address from the elevated to the ephemeral cf. Socrates' address of Strepsiades as 'Oh man of a day' in Aristophanes, *Clouds* 223.

934   *indulges* suggests that the man is too soft with himself and ought to restrain these lamentations. Note here how *mortem* is placed at the same point of this line as *mortalis* was in the previous one. The final monosyllable *fles* gives a strong emphasis to the word – Nature is (one might almost say) banging the table.

935-9   Nature argues that if he has enjoyed life so far, then he ought to be able to leave with good grace. One might feel that this ignores the natural human desire to prolong pleasure but Lucretius is presumably relying on the Epicurean principle that pleasure is the absence of pain and satisfaction of want. In which case 'infinite time contains the same amount of pleasure as finite time, if one measures the limits (of pleasure) by reason' (*Kuriai Doxai* 19) in that one can attain complete pleasure in a finite time and – as death is the total absence of all want – death (*securam quietem*) will be a continuation of this complete pleasure anyway. Lucretius does not spell this reasoning out explicitly here but relies instead on the rhetorical device of making the reader feel embarrassed at his greed and lack of good manners in overstaying his welcome and his needs at the banquet of life (938).

935   *anteacta priorque* is something of a tautology: 'past and done with'.

936-7   The image is an implicit myth referring to the tale of the daughters of Danaus, who murdered their husbands on their wedding night and were condemned to spend eternity filling jars with holes in them as a punishment. The image is thus of futility and lack of fulfilment; the Danaids will reappear at 1003-10. Note how Nature understates the case – 'if not *all* the pleasure of life...', i.e. 'if your life has not been *totally* wasted'. For the sense of *ingrata*, cf. Catullus 76.6, 9.

938   The line takes up the image of the maudlin banqueter from lines 912-18. The rhetorical impact is to make the reader ashamed of his bad manners in not knowing when it is time to leave; *plenus* is a neat touch, anticipating the Danaids' jars (which could never be filled) and applying the idea to the diner who is certainly 'full'. After a large banquet – which would take place from late afternoon to late night – the natural thing was to go home and sleep; the analogy with the sleep of death is thus irresistible.

939   The pressure is applied here: if death is 'rest' which is 'free from care' and to be entered into 'with contentment' (*aequo animo*), then only a fool (*stulte*) would object. The insult ('you fool') is thus no mere expletive but poised inbetween *securam* and *quietem* and is almost part of the argument – only a fool would object to 'rest free from cares'.

940-3   On the other hand, if life has been painful, then why seek to add to it?

940   The sentence structure reads: *si ea quaecumque es fructus periere profusa* ('if whatever you have enjoyed has all been poured out and perished'). The image of the leaking vessel is picked up from 936-7.

941   *in offensa esse* means 'to be hateful to' as in Cicero, *Letters to Atticus* 9.2a.2, usually referring to people but here used of life itself.

942   The recurrence of pain and futility is well brought out here: the repetition in *rursum*, the two words for 'dying' (*pereat...occidat*), the juxtaposed *male et ingratum* all rounded off with the generalised *omne*. There really is no cause for any optimism here.

943   The word *laboris* is rhetorically effective: putting an end to *labor* is an agreeable thing (cf. Catullus 31.7-11) and if life is *labor* then putting an end to it will also be agreeable. Note also the euphemistic *uitae finem facis* for 'die'; the poet is not here advocating suicide – the hypothetical situation is that the man is pleading to escape natural death.

944-5   The man might reply that life may hold out hope of improvement; to which Nature responds that 'all is always the same' (*eadem sunt omnia semper*) and so if the past was not pleasant then the future will be the same.

944   Nature is *rerum creatrix* and so might be expected to 'invent' something new for the jaded man.

945   *quod placeat* is a relative final clause – 'there is nothing which I could devise...which would please you'. 'All is always the same': the limits of variety are here depicted in stark terms and suggest that ultimately life would be too tedious to want to live any more.

946-7   The poet lightly alludes to the myth of Tithonus who was granted immortality by Zeus but was not given eternal youth; he consequently became weaker and weaker until he finally begged the gods to let him die. Notice here the repetition and variation in *marcet* ('wither' 'droop') and *languent* ('droop'), in *corpus* and *artus* and in the phrase *eadem tamen omnia restant* picking up *eadem sunt omnia semper*. The incessant prolongation of life is verbally brought out in his language.

948   'Even if you go on to outdo all living creatures in living'; *saeculum* is the perfect word here: it means 'a race of creatures' (OLD s.v. 'saeculum' 2) but also has a strong sense of 'a generation, lifetime'. Surpassing other creatures in the length of one's life – rather than, say, running or strength – is held up to ridicule.

949   The hyperbolic sequence is rhetorical: from being the longest-living man, to being the longest-living creature on earth, to being quite incapable of dying at all.

950-1   The poet uses the language of the lawcourts: *intendere* here means 'to bring a charge against' (OLD s.v. 'intendo' 13), *lis* is a lawsuit, *exponere* is the verb for 'setting out in words', *causam* is the 'case'. For the poet's use of legal language cf. 4.486-8. *naturam* is the subject of the infinitive *intendere*.

952-62 If Nature was reasonable with the younger man, she is now rude towards the old man who is still reluctant to face the inevitable. For the reluctance of the old to die, cf. Pheres' famous dictum at Euripides, *Alcestis* 691 ('you enjoy living – don't you think your father does too?') but contrast the words of the Laws of Athens to Socrates when he was facing execution as an old man (Plato, *Crito* 53d7-e2 'you are an old man, with only a short life left to you in all probability, yet you longed to live so greedily and contravened the greatest of laws – that is what everybody will say of you...').

952   *grandior* is a term of respect (see OLD s.v. 'grandis' 5) and connotes 'distinguished' and 'serious' as well as 'old'. Nature's rebuke is all the more pointed as a result.

953   *amplius aequo* means 'more than is reasonable'. Note the repetition of *queratur...lamentetur* and the spondaic rhythm of *lamentetur* as the old man whines.

955   Nature's remarks are comic in their rudeness towards this respected citizen. *baratre* is clearly a colloquial insult and its meaning still eludes scholars. It may be derived from the Greek word for a 'pit' and mean 'worth throwing into a pit'; or else a 'spendthrift' (who wishes to spend more life than he has); or it may be a corruption of *blatero* ('windbag'

	– unlikely, as his loquacity is not relevant and Nature may be rude but will not be crude); or else a corruption of *balatro* ('buffoon' – again, not really the image called for here).
956	*marces* picks up *marcet* from line 946.
957-8	The poet turns the argument into the familiar satirical image of 'discontent with one's lot' (*mempsimoiria* in Greek) as seen elsewhere at 3.1058-67 or Horace's famous line 'when in Rome I love Tibur, when in Tibur I love Rome, I as inconstant as the wind'. (*Epistles* 1.8.12: cf. *Satires* 2.7.28-9). Epicurus preached a philosophy of contentment and the poet constantly alludes to the way in which fear and ignorance rob us of the happiness which is freely available. The old man's discontent with what is to hand has made his whole life an unhappy time.
958-60	The final sentence of this section rounds it off effectively: we have a foretaste of the Danaids' water running out in *elapsast*, *ingrata* is picked up from line 942, death stands at his head just as the fearful man imagined himself standing at the head of his own corpse (883), and above all the words *satur et plenus* remind us of the image of life as a banquet. Kenney astutely remarks here that 'the *lectus* on which the old man lies is at once dining-couch and bier; and the one becomes the other before he is aware what is happening to him' (Kenney [1971] 218). The image is of death appearing unexpectedly before the man has had his fill of the feast: *nec opinanti* agrees with *tibi*.
961	'Unbefitting to your age' assumes that the old should accept death philosophically.
962	'Give way to the years' is a neat expression for 'surrender to the demands of time'.
963	A rhetorical line with repetition of *iure* and three increasingly lengthy verbs (*agat, increpat, inciletque*) asserts the poet's agreement with the sentiments of Nature.
964-71	All generations have to die to make room for the next one; death, it might be said, is the price we pay for sex.
964-5	*nouitate* is contrasted with *uetustas: cedit...necesse est* picks up the phrase *concede...necessest* in line 962. The sequence of generations is verbally brought out in the polyptoton *aliis aliud*.
966	The human being does not continue to exist in the underworld but the atoms of which he is composed go to make new human beings. This manages to reassure the reader that the popular superstitions about life after death are false as well as planting the seed of an idea which the next section will elaborate allegorically (978-1023). The phrase *barathrum nec Tartara...atra* is a hendiadys for 'the black pit of Tartarus'.

967 The construction of *opus est* + ablative is common enough (cf. 2.20-1); here the phrase takes the nominative ('matter is a need', i.e. matter is needed).

968 These future generations for whom you are making way will also themselves die: this is to allay any feelings of envy towards the younger generations. *uita perfuncta* means 'when they have finished with life'.

969 The endless succession of death is well brought out by the juxtaposition of *cecidere cadentque* – they have died and they will die. The line (imitated later by Horace [*Ars* 70]) is somewhat confusing to read: Lucretius seems to be saying that all ages will die – and that ages before you have already died: 'the ages before this no less than you have died – and will die'. The phrasing gives the impression of a random succession of births and deaths in which tense-distinctions (of past and future) which matter to us will all be relative to the universal nature of death.

970-1 As often in Lucretius, the first line of the couplet explains the point simply and the second line places the idea in a legal metaphor of great power and memorability. *mancipium* is full and complete legal possession of property, whereas *usus* is the right to use property for a temporary period. There is no exact English equivalent, but one might compare the distinction between renting and buying property. Notice here the contrast also of *nulli* and *omnibus*.

972-7 This repeats the point made forcefully at 832-42 and gives a sense of closure to the passage: the lines echo and repeat the earlier passage in fact, just as time after death reflects time before birth. The image of time before birth and time after death being a 'reflection' is excellent.

972 *respice* is addressed to the reader: *quam* here means 'how'.

973 *quam nascimur ante* here = *antequam nascimur*. Once again the present tense is used to show how the past (*anteacta*), present and *futuri* are one and all *nil ad nos*.

974 *speculum* is a 'reflection' or a 'mirror-image', whereby eternal past mirrors eternal future but all add up to zero.

975 *denique* has the sense of finality 'after our eventual death'.

976-7 A series of three rhetorical questions. The first two point to the lack of anything unpleasant in death and use parallel verbs *apparet* and *uidetur* and parallel adjectives *horribile* and *triste*. The final question uses (suitably soporific) assonance of *omni somno* and 's' alliteration (cf. Virgil, *Aeneid* 4. 81) and ends on a note of Epicurean *ataraxia* in the key word *securius* (meaning 'free from *cura*').

978- 'Why this is Hell, nor am I out of it.' The myths of the underworld
1023 explained as allegories of the unphilosophical life. The myths of the

Greeks placed certain arch-criminals in situations of eternal torment after death, and Lucretius uses four of these myths as material for his own 'remythologising' of the myths which his rationalism has discarded.

Tantalus is allegorised as showing the disabling power of the fear of the gods, Tityos is prostrate with the passion of love, Sisyphus is the ambitious politician who keeps failing, the Danaids are those who are never satisfied with what is available to them.

978-9 An opening general statement introducing what is to come. Acheron is a river in the underworld (6. 763) but the name is used in general for the underworld.

980-3 In Homer (*Odyssey* 11.582-92), Tantalus was punished for stealing the nectar and ambrosia of the gods by being put into a river with water up to his waist and fruit growing on trees above his head. Whenever he made to drink the water it receded from him, and the wind constantly blew the fruit out of his reach. This myth is thus an image of frustration. Lucretius however adopts a different version of the punishment, whereby a large rock was suspended over his head and he did not dare eat or drink for fear of it falling on him.

980 *impendens aere* means 'hanging in the air'.

981 *ut fama est* nicely distances the poet from his material. *cassa formidine* looks forward to *metus inanis* in the next line.

982-3 The image of Tantalus looking up to the stone is inverted to the fear of gods pressing down on mortal men; and Lucretius well uses the two meanings of *casus* as both specific 'falling' (of the rock) and generalised 'fortune'. Line 983 ends with a monosyllable which throws stress onto *fors* as the decisive agent in this process.

984 Tityos was a giant who tried to rape Leto and who was punished by having two vultures feeding on his liver, as told in Homer, *Odyssey* 11.576-81. The action of the vultures, here simply called 'birds', is understated as *ineunt* ('they go into him').

985-6 A difficult sentence: 'nor are they able (*possunt*) to find anything at all for them to probe within his massive chest for the whole of time'. However gigantic this giant's chest is, there is nothing for them to find – as none of this tale is true.

987-99 A related point: even if the tale were true, and no matter how massive the giant were, there would not be enough of him to keep the birds occupied for ever.

987 *proiectu* is apt for the giant's frame 'stretched out'. The whole line stresses his vast bulk: note the adjective *immani* ('huge'), and rare noun *proiectu*, the defining noun *corporis* ('body') and the verb *exstet* ('extend').

988-9   The repeated *qui* clauses here are concessive: 'let him occupy not only nine *iugera* with his limbs stretched out...but let him even occupy the whole earth, still (*tamen*) he will not be able...'. The *iugerum* was the standard measurement of land in Latin, very roughly equivalent to two thirds of an acre: so nine *iugera* will be about six acres. Line 989 is spondaic and slow in delineating the vast static mass of the giant's body.

990-1   The couplet is framed by words for eternity (*aeternum...semper*) which mark out the point being made. If nothing lasts for ever, then neither his pain nor the food will last for ever.

992-4   The allegorical interpretation is well discussed by Kenney (P.C.P.S. [1970]), who urges that the *uolucres* are the Cupids or 'loves' and so the giant, prostrate and devoured by birds, is like the lover who lies prostrate tormented by the winged Cupids. The language of *anxius angor* and *curae* here looks forward to the treatment of love in Book 4.

993-4   *exest* is from *exedo* and means 'devours'. The sequence of verbs is effective, *lacerant, exest, scindit*: just as the vultures tear open the skin, eat out the liver and split it open, and just as love 'torments' (OLD s.v. 'lacero' 3b), 'consumes with passion' and also 'tears apart' the happiness of the lover. *scindit* also has a sexual sense ('screw') as in Catullus 112.2 which is appropriate here. *curae* is nominative plural subject of *scindunt*. *cuppedine* is something of a wry joke if Kenney is right to say that the *uolucres* here are 'Cupids'.

995-1002   Sisyphus was punished by being forced to roll a large stone up to the top of a hill from which it always rolled down again. Here he is seen as allegorical for the politician, and the poet mocks the politician with his own vocabulary.

996   *fasces* and *secures* are the rods and axes which were the symbols of Roman political authority, here called 'brutal' to express some of the poet's distaste for political power as it was used and abused in Rome, and also to point a contrast between the savage power of the axes and the constant political impotence of Sisyphus. There is also mockery of what is being sought: not real power but the show of power, the empty symbols rather than real prosperity (cf. 3.78). *petere* is the politician's *mot juste* for 'standing for office'.

997   *imbibit* is an effective metaphor: 'thirsts for'. The line is framed by the two verbs, the one showing his deep desire, the other his sad departure. The wording is hyperbolic – not all politicians were always defeated or else nobody would ever have been elected, and there were some glorious political careers forged in Republican Rome.

998   The hyperbole continues: the man is never given power – and it would be worthless (*inane*) even if he did get it – and it causes him to endure unending toil. Note again that he 'never' gets power and 'always' endures toil.

999 The politician is prepared to endure 'hard labour', just as the fool in 3.62 was prepared to *niti praestante labore*.

1000-1 Note the heavy labouring spondees of line 1000 and the spondee *saxum* pushed over the line-end and poised to fall with the dactyl *quod tamen*.

1002 The *campus* here is both the plain onto which Sisyphus' rock rolled and in Rome the *Campus Martius* which was the place where the Roman people met to hold elections. Thus the stone rolls back to the plain; and the thwarted politician goes straight back to the *Campus* to seek re-election (*petit*) (cf. West 102).

1003-10 The Danaids have already been referred to in this book (936-7) and the poet now uses them as an image of 'discontent'. Unlike the previous myths, however, where he told the story and then presented the allegory, Lucretius here presents the moral allegory and then refers it to the myth of the Danaids.

1003-4 Kenney takes *numquam* with both *explere* and *satiare*, but the Roman reader would naturally understand the line as meaning: 'to fill it with good things but never satisfy it'. Note contrasting line-endings *semper... numquam*.

1005-6 The seasons bring us their different good things in sufficient quantity for all of us, and yet we are never satisfied with it all. The poet points out the eternal recurrence of good things (*redeunt*) – the crops themselves (*fetus, fructus*) and also the delightful appearance they present (*uarios lepores*): a beauty which is always there but often not noticed in the futile scramble for wealth. Note also how Lucretius modestly continues to include himself in the number of people who are unsatisfied (*nobis... explemur*).

1008-10 The poet cleverly links the Danaids with the theme of dissatisfaction: the girls are at 'a flowering time of life' reminding us of the fruitful seasons of lines 1005-7. *expleri* is a direct reminder of line 1004 and *nulla ratione* is of course ambivalent: 'in no way possible' as applied to the girls, but also 'by no amount of philosophy' as applied to the dissatisfied unenlightened people.

1011-23 The pains of hell are really the pains of conscience and the fear of punishment. If West is right (note on Hesiod, *Theogony* 119) that the name Tartarus derives from the Greek verb *tarasso* ('I disturb'), then this has added piquancy in that Epicurus' ideal state of contentment was *ataraxia* or 'lack of being disturbed') and so he can set up Tartarus as the enemy of *ataraxia*.

1011   Cerberus was the three-headed dog who guarded the entrance to the under-
world. The Furies were primeval beings (female in form with snakes in
their hair) who avenged crimes, especially crimes of bloodshed within
the family, as in Aeschylus' *Eumenides* (cf. Catullus 64.192-7 with my
note *ad loc*). For the proverbial 'lack of light' in the underworld, cf.
Homer, *Iliad* 8. 13, 478-81; Hesiod, *Theogony* 119. The phrase is philo-
sophically significant as Lucretius often regards ignorance and fear as
'darkness', and philosophy as 'light' (e.g. 1.144-5, 2.55-61 [= 3.87-93,
6.35-41]).

The line has occasioned much textual discussion as it contains no
verbs; this leaves the whole sentence lacking a verb, as the only ones
available are after the relative pronoun in 1013. There may be a line (or
group of lines) which has dropped out after 1011 – and later writers such
as Seneca and Servius seem to have read an account of Ixion in Lucretius
along with the sinners so far described. If Ixion has dropped out,
however, it will have been from the text of 978-1010 and this may not
help us in 1011-13. The lack of a connective after *egestas* has prompted
some editors to emend to *egenus* so that the phrase then reads 'Tartarus,
lacking in light' rather than 'the lack of light, Tartarus'. The absence of
a verb might also be corrected by reading *haec* for *qui* in line 1013. The
text printed is difficult and fraught with such problems, but the sense is
clear.

1012   The effective image of Tartarus 'belching' from his 'throat' horrible
fires (cf. 1.724) is clearly overstated as a caricature to be replaced with
the prosaic psychological truth.

1013   They do not exist and could not exist either.

1015   The verb *est* is strongly stressed at the start of the line: the torments of Tar-
tarus do not exist but fear *does* exist. Note the polyptoton of *insignibus
insignis* to suggest that the greater the crime the greater the fear. *scelerisque
luella* means 'paying for the crime', i.e. penalties set for wrongdoing.

1016-17 A terrifying list of punishments. The 'throwing down from the rock'
refers to the manner in which prisoners were flung from the Tarpeian
rock to their death. *uerbera* are 'beatings', *carnifices* are 'executioners'.
robur may mean the dungeon of the Mamertine prison called the
Tullianum, where such famous enemies of the Roman state as Jugurtha
and the Catilinarian conspirators were executed, but (if so) is perhaps
less effective after *carcer* and so may be better understood as referring
to the stocks (*eculeus*). 'Pitch, metal-plates and torches' were all used
in the torture of criminals by fire, or in executing them by burning at the
stake.

1018-19 The real torture is bad enough, but the human imagination can feed on this and invent its own torture. *sibi conscia factis* means 'guilty of its misdeeds'. The force of the prefix *prae* on *praemetuens* is that the mind is terrified before even being punished and so torments itself with the lash and the goad, which were both used in coercion of slaves and animals. Note here the two verbs: the mind *adhibet* the goads and 'scorches' itself with the lash; the effects of whipping would be the sort of inflamed redness which *torret* evokes, as well as the mental 'fever' of, for example, Horace, *Odes* 3.9.13.

1020-1 As often, the poet points out that philosophy could prevent this sort of excessive suffering by showing the man that there is a limit to the suffering available and that – even if such suffering here and now were unavoidable – death would bring a welcome release from it all. The superstitious man allows his knowledge of 'real-life' torture to let him invent more and worse things of the same kind after death. The key is to know the 'limits' of things (cf. 1.76-7, 595-6, 5.89-90, 6.65-6). In this case the *terminus* is death.

1023 'This is how the life of fools becomes hellish'. Having earlier not disassociated himself from the people who are unsatisfied with good things (1007), Lucretius now firmly distances himself from the 'fools' who, by fearing torture after death, render this life a hell on earth – in a nice example of a self-fulfilling prophecy or circular argument:

> I fear torture after death. This fear is itself a form of torment; therefore hell exists.

As often, the key to happiness is the removal of fear – and the key to that is knowledge.

Book Four

Lucretius has already discussed dreams as a form of mental illusion (453-61), and in particular singled out dreams of the dead several times to counter the superstitious belief in ghosts and fear of death. In this passage he is concerned to explain dreams in terms of images; dreams can thus be explained in naturalistic terms, without recourse to the supernatural explanations which are often put upon them (cf. Cicero, *de diuinatione* 1.63). This is why the poet later brings in animals dreaming, to counter the belief in the prophetic nature of dreams, which are in fact purely and simply the mechanical reaction of the mind to the images presented to it during the day. The passage here printed concerns itself largely with the 'occupational' dreams: Lucretius argues that our 'enthusiasm and pleasure'

(984) lead us, even in sleep, to focus on those images most familiar to us – or indeed most worrying to us, as in the case of dreamers indicting themselves in their sleep (1018-19), or dreamers terrified of imaginary wild beasts (1016-17). All of this rather contradicts Lucretius' earlier statement (765) that the memory lies dormant in sleep.

962-3	Lucretius distinguishes two causes of recurrent dreams: obsessional interest and the length of time spent on a given activity. Note the effective juxtaposition of words of 'binding' and then 'sticking' in *deuinctus adhaeret.*
963-5	The poet raises the stakes from *multum* to *magis* to *plerumque.*
964	*contenta magis* means here 'more intent' (M.F. Smith). The line ends with the final monosyllable in the alliterative *magis mens.*
966-70	The first three groups of dreamers are given a single line each, leading to the poet's own dreams which occupy two lines.
966	The repetition in *causidici causas* is the sort of etymological repetition found in 'the rhetorical style of the lawyer's courtroom' (Snyder, 79), followed by the repetition of ideas in *pugnare ac proelia obire* in the next line.
968	The archaism of *induperatores* (for *imperatores*) is Ennian, and makes the archaic reading *duellum* more certain.
969-70	Many poets claimed to have had poetic dreams (Callimachus, Ennius, Propertius). What distinguishes this dream is the naturalistic and realistic flavour of it in contrast to their supernatural fantasies. This poet dreams that he is still engaged in his daily activity of composing the *de rerum natura* (note the phrase *rerum...naturam* in 969). The significance of *patriis chartis* is to remind us that the poet is turning material from Greek into the Latin language (see 1.136-9).
973-83	This book employs a good deal of imagery from the theatre (cf. 74-83, 768-772, 788-93) and theatrical metaphors are still to come (1186). The theatre is in fact 'a small but fitting *leitmotif* in the book concerned with sense-perception' (Schrijvers [1980] 142). The theatre is both analogical to our perception of the world in general (e.g. in that we only see the surface façade of things) and also exemplifies features of our perception (e.g. colour) which the poet wishes to explain.
	Roman games lasted at least a week (*ludi Cereales*) if not two weeks (*ludi Romani*) and during the late Republic grew steadily longer (see Carcopino 224-5).
976	Lucretius attempts to explain the mechanics of short-term habit or memory in terms of specific channels (*uias*) opened up.

977　　The term *simulacra* is a technical term in Epicureanism for the visible 'films' which emanate from things and which are apprehended by the senses. For the full explanation, see 4.26-323; Sharples 12-19.

978　　*multos...dies* picks up *dies multos* in line 973. The argument here is *a fortiori*: if we see such 'dreams' even when awake (*etiam uigilantes*) then all the more will these images crowd our dreams.

981　　an appropriately musical line with chiastic sound pattern of *liquidum carmen chordasque loquentis*, the *c* alliteration suggesting the sound of the strings being plucked and the interchange of epithets with *liquidum* (more suitable for sound than words) leading to *loquentis* (more fitting for songs than strings).

983　　The reader is left with the dazzling dream-image of the theatre, with three words all denoting impressive sights (*uarios splendere decores*).

Sex and Love

Lucretius is pessimistic in the extreme about certain forms of Romantic Love, and at the end of Book 4 he feels impelled to spend a great deal of time attacking this particular form of madness.

First let us examine Epicurus', rather ambivalent, attitude to the subject. In one place he says:

> sexual intercourse has never done a man good, and he is lucky if it hasn't done him harm　　　　　　　　　　(Diogenes Laertius 10.118)

whereas elsewhere (Diogenes Laertius 10.6) he counts sexual pleasure among the good things of life. The Epicurean ideal was *ataraxia* (serenity and contented freedom from all disturbance) and so sexual activity will be good if it promotes this by removing the pain of frustration, but bad if it impairs the overall serenity of the wise man's disposition. The wise man therefore is not to fall in love but neither is he necessarily to remain celibate.

Lucretius makes it abundantly clear that the sexual urge is natural: Book 4 has argued that perception is the result of effluences beyond our control, and he explains the experiences of hunger, sleep and dreams in strictly atomic terms. When sex is introduced, therefore, it is in a context of mechanical atomic reactions over which we have little or no control: just as Aristotle (*de motu animalium* 703b5ff) discusses the movement of the penis, along with sleeping and waking and breathing, as movements over which we have no control (see Furley, *Two Studies in the Greek Atomists* 221-2). Lucretius describes the noctural emission of sperm after the (superficially similar) phenomenon of bedwetting – both examples of involuntary actions. The emission of sperm is both natural and necessary, what is unnatural and unnecessary is the behaviour of the romantic lover.

Lucretius emphasises this dichotomy of the *sani* and the *miseri*: the healthy people who use food and sex but are literally under no illusions about either, and the diseased wretched people who do not. The pathetic delusions of the infatuated lover are described (1068-9) as a sore and then as madness, whereas the quieter charms of the 'homely little woman' are enunciated with approval and the 'habit of love' sounds more like Epicurean friendship (1278-87). Sexual pleasure fell into the class of pleasures which are natural but not necessary, and hence are to be satisfied where necessary, but not indulged in beyond the body's natural need (Diogenes Laertius 10.127, Cicero, *de finibus* 1.45). Once again it is axiomatic that pleasure, once the immediate desire has been satisfied, can only be varied and not increased, especially if we are considering this sort of kinetic pleasure which only arises from mechanical causes and thus is simply a response to an involuntary stimulus. The sexual urge is inborn in us, to be awakened when we enter the choppy tides of adolescence (4.1030); perception is the result of effluences beyond our control, and hunger, sleep and dreams are all explicable in similarly mechanistic atomic terms. The creation and emission of sperm is thus natural; what is unnatural and unecessary is the retention of sperm as practised by the romantic lover for whom no other woman will do, whose sheer frustration causes him to idealise the beloved and project his fantasies onto her. The locked-out serenader would flee if he were actually admitted and his illusions about the girl were rudely shattered (4.1177-84). Marriage is assumed (4.1277) and even recommended with a wife who has 'compliant ways and bodily cleanliness' (4.1281), whereas the romantic lover is doomed to frustration: his obsessive attachment to one girl will limit his chances of obtaining sexual pleasure compared to the chances enjoyed by the promiscuous, where the girl may not be beautiful but she is certainly better than nothing (a nice example of the *paruum quod satis est* argument, also found at 2.20-36, 5.1412-35).

Lucretius' attitude can thus be seen to be descriptive rather than prescriptive: the romantic lover does not in fact enjoy the life of love, as it does not answer the bodily needs which sexual pleasure serves. The romantic lover's attitude to sex is blind, greedy and unsatisfied – the perfect antithesis of the Epicurean ideal of open-eyed moderate pleasure. It is these unhealthy aspects of love which Epicurus and Lucretius condemn, rather than the simple fulfilment of bodily need and the consequent kinetic pleasure to be derived from it. Sexual love is simply a function of the animal body; it does not give our life any meaning in itself.

1058-60 The final word of the previous line is *cupido* ('desire'), which is also the name in mythology of Venus' winged son who fires arrows of love at his victims. Note here the tricolon crescendo of *haec...hinc...hinc*, and the slightly pejorative tone of *illaec* ('that old cliché of...') introducing the idea of love dripping into the heart, only to freeze. Fitzgerald suggests that Lucretius is thinking of a stalagmite growing upwards (*successit*) from underneath dripping water. *cura* – a word often used in love poetry to allude to the beloved herself – is here hardly flattered by the adjective *frigida*.

1061   The Epicurean theory of perception, as expounded earlier in Book 4, dooms the lover to perpetual teasing from the beloved. Nor are these the changing images from 'any and every body' (1032), as *illius* lingers on in wistful enjambement and her name is singular and 'sweet' (cf. Propertius 1.12.6)

1063   The metaphor of *pabula* is picked up in 1068 (*alendo*). Again, Lucretius translates the poetic *amoris* into the prosaic *umorem* (1065) – we should flee *amor* by expelling *umor*.

1065-7   Lucretius sees romantic love as born of sexual frustration; the lover's physical desire is transmuted into an idealisation of the beloved. This is corroborated later on by the figure of the *exclusus amator* ('locked-out lover') whose devotion relies on his not being admitted and thereby disillusioned.

1065   *in corpora quaeque* suggests promiscuous sex (as later in line 1071). The indiscriminate sowing of wild oats seems to have been recommended to young males even by the stern Cato (see Porphyry on Horace, *Satires* 1.2) who approved of the young frequenting the brothel. See Lyne (1980) 1-4.

1067   Epicureans regarded pleasure as what we all seek and pain as to be avoided; this pain of sexual frustration is 'certain' in that it is a mechanical response to the lover's behaviour. Lucretius will develop the theme (1080-2) when describing how the pain of love can drive lovers to inflict pain on each other.

1068   The notion of love as a disease has a long history in classical literature: Sophocles, *Trachiniae* 445, Euripides, *Hippolytus* 477, Catullus 76.20, etc. However, what in those authors is a metaphor is here far more literally meant in a situation where bodily behaviour (albeit psychologically conditioned) causes bodily pain and sickness.

1069   *furor* is a key word and lends coherence to the book as a whole. The essence of madness to the Greeks was hallucination: one thinks of Sophocles' Ajax killing the cattle while thinking that they were the Greek generals, Euripides' Heracles killing his wife and children believing them to be the family of his enemy, both cases where the madness is the mistaken perception and not the violent anger itself. In this book which has explained true perception and pushed for the reliability of the senses, the poet ends with a picture of the sad consequences of the lover's failure to see the beloved as she really is, a scathing satire on the lover's euphemisms for her physical defects (1160-70) and a mocking scenario of the lover being granted his desire only to see its true worthlessness (1180-91).

1070 Effective phrasing, which puts *prima* next to *nouis*, emphasises the urgency of striking as soon as the wounds of love appear.

1071 Lucretius uses a compound adjective *uolgiuagus* (probably taken from Callimachus' *periphoitos* [*Ep.* 28.3]), which is immediately strengthened by *uagus* which follows it.

1072 Epicurus himself advised this: 'remove sight and...contact and the passion of love is ended' (*Sent. Vat.* 18).

1073-4 Casual sex has none of the penalties attached to it which Lucretius outlines in lines 1121-40, and is thereby more conducive to pleasure than romantic attachment. The pleasure is *pura* – uncontaminated by illusions and futile expectations. Lucretius contrasts the healthy (*sanis*) with the sick (*miseris*) continuing the idea of 'pain' in 1067, the 'sore' in 1068 and the 'wounds' in 1070. Similar praise of casual sex is found in Horace, *Satires* 1.2, 2.7.

1077-8 Lucretius presents a comic picture of the lover spoilt for choice, unable to decide what to enjoy first and so not enjoying any of it properly. The metaphor of 'burning' in *ardor* is extended below at 1086-7. Cf. also 1.473-7, where the fire of Paris' passion for Helen led to the real fire of Troy being sacked.

1079-81 Lucretius' language is deliberately provocative, interweaving the affectionate words of love (the diminutive *labellis*; *oscula*) with verbs of violence (*dentes inlidunt* having the right dental sounds and also a loud repetition of *dent...-dunt*, the phrase being more at home in the boxing match of Virgil, *Aeneid* 5.480). The romantic notion of the love-bite (as in Catullus 8.18) is transformed into something far more neurotic and unhealthy. *oscula* is common in love-poetry to mean 'kisses' but here means 'mouths' which crash together (*adfligunt* – again a term more fitting for a head-butt).

1082 *stimuli* is a wonderful touch; the lover is 'hurt' into love-making in which he hurts his beloved in a vicious circle of pain. The phrase also suggests the slavery of love, as the 'mistress' tortures him like an animal – the goad was a stick with a sharp point on the end used to stir lethargic animals into action (cf. 3.874n). Note also the impersonal word *id* – the lover is blind in his helpless addiction to his love.

1083	*rabies* is a stronger word than *furor* (1069).
1085	*refrenat* is a metaphor from horse-riding. Venus controls the love-bites so that they are still pleasurable.
1089-90	The desire for food and drink is caused by a physical need which can be satisfied. The mere build-up of sperm can also easily be satisfied (1030-6). What cannot be satisfied is the extravagant hope of the infatuated lover caricatured at lines 1110-12.
1093	The phrase *laticum frugumque cupido* is Homeric in sound (cf. Homer, *Iliad* 1.469) and combines with *facile* to suggest the age-old ease of satisfying hunger and thirst.
1094	*facie* and *colore* are merely superficial aspects of a human being, with *facies* referring to bodily appearance in general and not only the face (*uoltus*). Images only communicate shape and colour, after all (cf. 4. 243).
1096	*tenuia* is stressed by the enjambement and the following pause.
1097-	A highly effective simile. The key-word *umor* is used again to link this
1100	with sex – the play on words contrasting *umor* and *amor*. *simulacraque petit frustraque laborat* is a relentless catalogue of futility (images are insubstantial, he is seeking (but not finding them), it is in vain and he is 'labouring'). The thirst itself (*sitit*) is placed in the middle of the river (*medioque...torrenti*) and the poet teases the reader with *potans* poised at the end of the line (the man is drinking and yet he is still thirsty).
1102-14	The lover wishes not merely to enjoy but also to possess the body of the beloved. Lucretius caricatures this with the ludicrous picture of lovers removing parts of the body or attempting to disappear inside the lover's body.
1103	The juxtaposition of *teneris abradere* heightens the effect.
1105-6	The metaphor of *flore...aetatis* is a nice euphemism. Cf. 1038, OLD s.v. 'flos' 8a.
1107	*conserat arua* is a less euphemistic phrase (cf. 1272-3, Adams 82-5).
1108-11	After the metaphors, Lucretius now becomes very specific. The singular *corpus* may suggest the unity of the two bodies into one, *auide...saliuas* certainly connotes the idea of eating greedily (cf. 1091-1100), and the quasi-medical specificity of *iungunt saliuas oris* lends an ironic distance to the description. The notion of getting 'right inside that body' is then the language of comic excess and exaggeration.
1115	*cupido* ('desire') is here metonymic for 'sperm'.
1116	Note the juxtaposition of *ardoris uiolenti* and the alliteration of *p*.
1118	The subjunctive in *quod cupiant* is a final clause ('something to desire') – for which cf. Ovid, *ars am.* 1.35 (*quod amare uelis reperire labora*).
1120	Love as a disease again (cf. 1068) and now blind as well as dumb (1057): *caecus* meaning both 'blind' and also 'unseen'.

1121-40 The price of love. It is obvious that Lucretius is here referring to obsessive 'romantic' love which takes over the lover's whole life, and his condemnation of it is couched in terms comparable to those of Cicero (*pro Caelio* 42) whose view is that love is *otium* – fine in its place but not to interfere with *negotium*.

1122 The phrase *sub nutu degitur aetas* suggests the 'slavery of love' by which later love-poets adopted the stance of self-abasement before the 'mistress' (see Lyne [1979], Kenney [1970] 389), but Lucretius would surely have spelt this idea out more fully if such a notion were common in his own time. It would have (after all) been a gift for his argument that romantic love debases and causes pain – as indeed it would have been for the Horace of *Satires* 1.2. The lover in this passage is wholly obsessed with one woman and so is entirely dependent on her whims and feelings. There is a touch of the indignity found in, for example, Heracles being enslaved to the woman Omphale, and the atomist philosopher Democritus also expressed the opinion that 'the worst insult for a man would be to be governed by a woman' (DK B111). The matter is raised to a higher level by the word *nutu* which strongly suggests the all-powerful nodding of the head as practised by Zeus in Homer (e.g. *Iliad* 1.524-7, an action which rules the universe); *aetas* also suggests that the man is squandering his youth in the obsessive pursuit of a woman.

1123-40 This passage is the stuff of Roman comedy: the young man in love wasting his father's money, or squandering his ancestors' fortunes. There are many parallels in Roman comedy for the young man wasting money on a girlfriend, e.g. Terence, *Ad.* 117, Plautus, *Mostellaria* 295.

1123 Cf. 4.1029. Babylonian cloth was fabulously coloured and expensive.

1124 Lucretius suggests that the lover allows his sense of duty and responsibility to dwindle over a period of time.

1125 The metaphor *rident* is highly appropriate in the case of the man being mocked by the gifts he buys his girlfriend. For Sikyon as the source of expensive slippers, see A. Griffin (1982) 32 n.2. Lucian (*Dial. Mer.* 14.2) tells us that they cost two drachmas, which was the price of 'two nights with a call-girl'.

1127 *thalassina* only occurs here and clearly refers to the crimson 'purple' dye obtained from the shellfish *murex brandaris*.

1128 After the *haute couture* of lines 1125-7, the poet surprises us with the bathetic tone of 1128: the obsessive lover (and *assidue* suggests obsession) soon finds his finery tattered and sweaty.

1129 *anadema* is only found here and is clearly a transliteration of a Greek word, close to the word *diadema* which was a headband decorated with jewels and gold. Cf. Paoli 106; and for the mood of this passage, compare *Palatine Anthology* 5.199.

1130 The manuscripts read *atque Alidensia* and this has been taken by most editors as referring to Alinda in Caria; the reading is highly suspect, however. Firstly, the name Alinda would not give us an adjective *alidensus* with no 'n', and secondly, there is no evidence of Alinda producing anything but olives, and certainly not textiles. Lambinus' proposal *Melitensia* ('Maltese') is far more plausible, as Maltese cloth is mentioned in Cicero (*Verrines* 2.176, 4.103; cf. Diodorus Siculus 5.12.2). Maltese cloth probably had the erotic transparency of the more famous 'Coan garments', and the reading *Coa* is here adopted in place of the manuscript reading *Chia* for the simple reason that garments from Cos were renowned in the Roman world as the designer-label for the well-dressed young woman, while Chios is not known for such material. The notorious transparency of the Coan garments (cf. Horace, *Satires* 1.2.101-2, Tibullus 2.4.29, Propertius 4.2.23, Horace, *Odes* 4.13.13, Griffin (1985) 10 and n.91) is especially appropriate in this book, concerned above all with sense-perception, and in this passage – which is arguing that the lover needs to *see* the truth about his beloved; and the besotted lover cannot do this even when she is totally visible (to everybody else) through her clothes.

1131-2 The poet builds up the catalogue of expenditure by the use of asyndeton, thus stressing the waste and also the lover's irrational obsession. Lucretius elsewhere (5. 1412-35) inveighs against the futile pursuit of increased pleasure through luxury, but in this passage he is rather showing how the lover – despite his massive expense and accumulation of 'pleasures' – will still not achieve happiness.

1133 The image of the spring reminds us of Plato's *Phaedrus* 255c, in which the fountain of desire flows from beloved to lover and back again.

1134 *amari* ('bitter') is a play on words, reminding us of *amari* ('to be loved').

1136 *lustris* are 'brothels': Lucretius is not saying that all mistresses were prostitutes in brothels; there was a large assortment of women to choose from (see Lyne [1980] 8-17) ranging from the slave-prostitute to the high-class non-citizen courtesan freedwoman. Roman opinion did not condemn the use of brothels (cf. 1065n). For the sense of *perire* (to 'perish' and also to 'love to distraction'), see Catullus 45.5.

1137 *iaculata* reminds us of the imagery of the 'warfare of love' (*militia amoris*) as at 1050-1. Here, instead of Cupid firing love, we have the mistress firing doubt and misery, a debunking of the romantic myth of Cupid's arrow in a cynical scenario: 'the real "arrows" in love are like this'.

1140   Cf. 1125n; and note the alliteration of initial *u*.

1145-50 The hunting metaphors are prominent here, although they are surprisingly uncommon in earlier Greek poetry, except in the genre of the Hellenistic Epigram (cf., for example, *Palatine Anthology* 5.64.4, 12.87. 5-6). 'These "snares of love", familiar in the worthless poetry with which some of his readers must be presumed to be excessively familiar, really existed and were dangerous.' (Kenney [1970] 388.)

1150   *tibi obstes* here means 'stand in your own way' and is a colloquialism.

1153   *caeci* is one of the key words of the section and the book. It is the inability to see what is there which fetters the lover, and so the first prerequisite for sanity is simply to look.

1155   *prauas turpisque* is strong language. *prauus* denotes deformity (mental and physical) and sits provocatively with *in deliciis* (how can 'sweethearts' be disgusting?), just as *turpis* (disgraceful to be seen with) is hardly fitting for one *in honore*. The 'deformity' is to the lover a 'darling', the 'slut' is a queen. Note again the poised verb *uidemus*.

1157-8 The besotted lovers offer each other advice on the idiocy of their loves, oblivious to their own folly. *adflictentur* has the senses of sickness and also military harassment (OLD s.v. 'afflicto' 1b, 2a).

1160-70 A famous catalogue of euphemisms. The sceptic philosopher Sextus Empiricus (*O.P.* 1.108) remarks that 'many men who have ugly girlfriends think them highly attractive' as part of his argument that different people may make different judgements about the same sense-experience. Lucretius turns this argument into a striking piece of satire, picking up an idea found in Plato (*Republic* 474d). Note here the lovers' use of Greek terms for the blunt Latin of Lucretius – Greek words being current in Rome along with many other expressions of Hellenism, as Martial (10.68. 5) and Juvenal (e.g. 3.58-125) were later to bemoan. For Lucretius' attitude towards Greek language, see Bailey (1947) 1.138-9 and Sedley (1999).

1160   *melichrus* is Greek for 'honey-gold', *acosmos* for 'unadorned'.

1161   *caesia* means 'grey-green' and here refers to the girl's eye-colour. The goddess Pallas Athene is often described as having this colour eyes (e.g. Cicero, *de natura deorum* 1.83) and so the lover flatters his beloved that she resembles the 'statue of Pallas'.

1162   *chariton mia* is Greek for 'one of the Graces'. *sal* means literally 'salt', but is used also to mean 'wit' (as at Catullus 13.5, 86.4).

1164   *traulizi* properly means to pronounce 'r' as 'l' (as in Aristophanes' *Wasps* 44). *balbus* denotes any speech impediment.

1165   *lampadium* (a diminutive form of the Greek *lampas*, 'lamp') only occurs here.

1168   Iacchus is a cult title for Bacchus, god of wine and known also as Liber. Cicero (*de natura deorum* 2.62) states he was born of Ceres, the goddess of corn.

1169   *philema* is again transliterated Greek for 'kiss'.

1171-6   Lucretius continues with an exaggerated attack on the girl – indeed the poet seems to be as irrational in his contempt for her as the lover is infatuated. The style imitates that of the *consolatio* and also the diatribe, with its twin weapons of parody mixed with quasi-realistic cynicism; the 'locked-out lover' (*exclusus amator*) is parodied and then the superficial charms of the woman are shown up as very much only skin-deep.

1171   *oris honore* has a pleasing assonance.

1172   The phrasing is hyperbolic, parodying the extravagant claims made for the girl by her lover; cf. Catullus 86.5-6.

1173-6   The three points of the *consolatio* for unrequited love are brought out by the tricolon crescendo, each phrase in the triad emphasised by the anaphora of *nempe*: the second point (we lived without her before) is very similar to the comment on death (we have been dead before we were born and it was not so bad: 3. 832-7). The third point (she is not worth it anyway) is stock 'sour grapes' reasoning, but neatly positioned to lead into the extended satire of the woman and her lover.

1175-6   What are the foul smells? Housman (1972) thought it referred to farting – which would explain the giggling maids and their hurried flight.

1177   The figure of the 'locked out lover' (*exclusus amator*), familiar from later love-elegy (Propertius 1.16.17-44, Tibullus 1.2, Ovid, *Amores* 1.6; see also Horace, *Odes* 1.25, 3.10 and Copley *passim*) and satirised in Horace, *Epode* 11.20-2 (where see Mankin *ad loc.*). It is often argued that the present passage would have no point if such behaviour were not a part of real life – Lucretius would hardly tilt at the windmill of a purely 'literary' phenomenon.

Notice here the variation in the poet's description: three different words for doors or parts of doorways (*limina...postes...foribus*); and three matching sets of actions: covering with flowers and garlands, smearing with marjoram (where the specificity of marjoram lends immediacy to the picture) and finally planting kisses on the door. The cartoon-like tone is enhanced by the transferred epithet of *superbos* set against *miser* in the next line – the woodwork is snooty while the lover grovels outside.

1180   The juxtaposition of the two participles *ammissum uenientem* adds a cinematographic swiftness and immediacy to the lover's entry and immediate disgust which are worth keeping. He has been admitted (perfect tense) and is on his way in (present tense) when....

1182 The short word *cadat* is most effective here, poised in the middle of the pompous *meditata diu...alte sumpta querela*. For all the time he has spent on it and for all the deep sincerity of his lament, he drops it in the space of two short syllables. *querela* is parody of the lover's affectations – it is used at 4.548 of the plaintive song of birds.

1184 *mortali concedere* is precisely what Lucretius recommends at 1191 (*humanis concedere rebus*).

1185 The use of the name Venus to mean 'mistress' is paralleled in Horace, *Odes* (1.27.14, 1.33.14) and Virgil (*Eclogues* 3.68). It remains an unusual, arch expression, however, ideal for the infatuated lover (Virgil) or the ironic commentator (Horace and Lucretius). Just how divine they are is precisely the point being explored.

1186 *postscaenia* occurs only here and fits very well with Lucretius' other theatrical allusions in this book (74-83, 768-72, 788-93). The point that the women are merely actresses, with their lovers willingly suspending disbelief, is made with the utmost economy. As in the theatre, the illusion remains only until one looks behind the scenery.

1189 *lucem* is a key theme. The romantic lover's illusions are a form of superstition (regarding women as gods etc.) which it is Lucretius' purpose to 'drag into the light' of reason. *risus* probably refers back to the giggling of line 1176.

1190-1 The colloquial *bello* is in deliberate contrast to the high-flown language of the lover; the man of common sense sees the girl as she is, in everyday language, unlike the romantic who dresses her obvious faults in pretentious euphemisms (1160-70). From this point on Lucretius gives concrete and positive advice on marital happiness in a manner shocking only to those who see him as a psychotic misogynist.

Book Five

The opening of this book (like Books 3 and 6) is taken up with praise of Epicurus, although the great man is not named. The argument here is that Epicurus deserves more praise than other 'benefactors' of mankind, both divine (Ceres and Bacchus) and semi-divine (Hercules). Costa ([1984] 51-2) describes its sardonic and hyperbolic qualities:

> It is a sardonic passage, with the labours ironically described in turgid and inflated language: *Nemeaeus magnus hiatus* 24, *uenenatis uallata colubris* 27, *tripectora tergemini uis Geryonai* 28...the series of questions beginning with *quid* 24 is finally answered bluntly and unequivocally with *nil, ut opinor* 39.

The case is made all the more convincing by the mock epic language and the denigrating tone of *Arcadius sus*, the redoubled trebles of *tripectora tergemini* (*tripectora* only occurs here), the sarcastic *spirantes naribus ignem*, the tricolon crescendo of *asper, acerba tuens, immani corpore serpens* appropriately building up the monster in layer upon layer of language, the geographical exactitude of line 31, and so on. The argument is bluntly and cruelly put: these monsters would be dead by now, and Hercules is not with us to rid us of the monsters which now need shooting, and these monsters live in places where nobody with any sense would go anyway. Once again, the world of 'heroic' myth and legend is sent up by its own style and subverted in the interests of philosophy; the myth is left in place as a poetic construct but its subject is held up to Epicurean *ratio* and found wanting. Similarly, the idea of Ajax killing cattle in deluded hallucination thinking that they were the Greek chiefs whose death was deserved because of a dispute over glory – all this would be rendered quite ludicrous on Epicurean principles; just as is the sacrifice of Iphigeneia to make the gods send wind.

1	The question sounds like a *cri de coeur* from one who is trying to compose just such a *carmen* himself, as well as being an imitation of Ennius, *Annales* frag. 164 Skutsch ('quis potus ingentis oras euoluere belli?'). *potis est* means simply 'is able'; *pollenti pectore* goes with it ('with heart strong') but looks forward to *pectore* in line 5 – Epicurus could produce such wonderful things from his *pectus* that the poet's *pectus* is hard pressed to match it. The question suggests on the surface that 'nobody' could match the achievement of Epicurus in verse, but leaves open the poet's real aspiration to do exactly that.
2	*condere* here means 'to compose' or 'construct' (OLD s.v. 'condo' 12). *pro* is to be taken after *dignum* ('a song worthy of the majesty of nature'). 'These discoveries' are the results of Epicurus' search for the truth (*quaesita praemia:* cf. 1.72-7).
3-4	After *quis potis est* we are now asked *quis ualet*, the contruction is 'who is so strong (*tantum ualet*) in words as to be able to..?'; *laudes/ pro meritis* go together: praise where praise is richly due.
5	*parta* and *quaesita* are inverted from the natural order, a device known as *husteron proteron*, perhaps to provide the strong alliteration of 'p'.
6	The catechism-like answer comes back in all modesty from the poet: nobody mortal is capable of doing justice to Epicurus. At this point 'nobody mortal' simply sounds like 'nobody at all' but the note of 'mortal' will lead on to the declaration of Epicurus' divine status in line 8.
7-8	'If we must speak as the known greatness of the universe demands, then (we must declare) he was a god....' The notion of declaring Epicurus a

god sounds odd to modern ears and merits some explanation. Certainly Lucretius (like Epicurus himself) believed that gods exist but that they take no part in our lives, living an immortal existence free of all care and anxiety. If these gods were capable of being bothered by human concerns then they would not enjoy the divine tranquillity which is theirs (see 3. 18-27). Epicurus died and so is hardly to be reckoned one of these immortal beings. How then was he a god? In the first place, Lucretius claims that if one follows the philosophy of Epicurus then it is possible to live a life 'worthy of the gods' (3. 322), just as the master himself asserted ('you will live as a god among men'; Epicurus, *Letter to Menoeceus* 135); and as Epicurus attained the state of complete contentment (*ataraxia*) enjoyed by the gods, then he was living such a 'divine' life. In the second place, Epicurus changed people's lives even more than the 'real' gods, as this passage is about to describe: Ceres and Bacchus gave us corn and wine, but neither of them is essential to happiness whereas Epicurus' philosophy transforms us from cowering malcontents into gods. The ancient concept of deification admitted the possibility of declaring a mortal a god, especially if he had the power of life and death over other human beings – hence the 'divinity' of Alexander the Great and even some Roman provincial governors – and this passage looks forward to mention of Hercules who was the most famous case of a mortal being promoted to Olympus. This was partly the belief that such great men owed their greatness to divine help, from which it was but a short step to the belief that these men actually possessed divine powers (see Ogilvie [1969] 119-23). The declaration here of Epicurus' divinity (stressed by the repetition of *deus*) is thus both orthodox and provocative, a paradox which forces the reader to think through the implications.

  inclute is a term elsewhere only used of Venus (1.40) and Epicurus (3.10). The address here rounds off the laudatory line well with the reminder that if the Master is divine, the addressee is also 'noble' and 'renowned'.

9   *princeps* here means little more than *primus* ('who was first to') but carries the sense of 'chief' as well as 'earliest in time' (see OLD s.v. 'princeps' 5). Epicurus is praised as the 'first discoverer' of the *ratio* of life to which we owe our salvation from misery and fear (cf. 1.66, 3.2, 6.4). Epicurus was not actually the first to discuss the atomic theory (which had been first invented by the fifth-century philosophers Democritus and Leucippus), but he did construct a philosophy of life out of this scientific doctrine. The word *inuenit* is carefully chosen: Epicurus did not 'fabricate' a theory but rather 'discovered' the true workings of life.

For Lucretius the ideas of Epicurus are not merely one alternative among a range of ideas but the only ones which are true.

10   *sapientia* is what the Romans call it; Epicurus, being Greek, called it *sophia*. *per artem* is also important: Epicurus did not merely stumble upon the truth by accident, his philosophy was expounded and developed by 'skill'.

11-12   The metaphor here is of the ship at sea in massive waves and darkness being moored safely in the harbour of peace and light. The storm and fear of line 11 are vividly evoked out by the alliteration of 't' and the repetition of *tantis*, with little life (*uitam*) lost in the middle of the words for the gigantic waves and darkness, while the peace of the harbour employs soothing 'l' sounds and assonance of 'a'. The couplet is symmetrical, with *fluctibus* answered by *tranquillo* and *tenebris* answered by *luce* at similar places in the lines. For the metaphor of storm/calm, cf. 2.15, 3.1-2; for the frequent use of the dark/light dichotomy expressive of ignorance/knowledge, see 2.54-61.

13   This line leads the reader into the next section of the poem, comparing the achievements of Epicurus with those of Ceres, Bacchus and Hercules. *reperta* is a passive participle but here stands for a noun ('discoveries').

14-15   *fertur* ('is said to have') distances the poet from his statement: no real Epicurean god would have disturbed his *ataraxia* by giving mortals anything. Note the alliteration of 'f' and then 'l'. 'Liber' is an alternative name for Bacchus, the Roman equivalent of the Greek god Dionysus, later on being used as a metonymy for 'wine' itself. The poet could have said *uinum* for 'wine' but chose to use the periphrasis 'the liquid of vine-born juice' as a parody of 'the priestly utterance, with *uitigeni* a parody of the cult title so dear to the *uates* whom Lucretius detested' (West [1969] 28).

16   *cum* here means 'although' and the sentence runs 'life could remain without these things'.

17   Lucretius is thinking of the Germans whose diet consisted of milk, cheese and meat (Caesar *BG* 6.22.1).

18   Man can live happily without certain sorts of food and drink, but not without a *puro pectore*. This is no circular argument ('one needs happiness to be happy') – the term *bene uiuere* connotes 'prosperity' as well as 'happiness' while *puro pectore* must mean 'with a heart purged (of fears)'. The idea was commonplace in Epicurean thought: cf. Epicurus, *Letter to Menoeceus* 132 'one cannot live pleasantly without also living sensibly and respectably and justly'.

19-21   The sentence rounds off the passage by explaining the divinity of Epicurus. *quo magis* means 'and so all the more', *merito* means 'rightly'.

20   The 'great nations' through which Epicureanism has spread are Greece and Italy; in both Epicureanism was one of the most influential philosophies, competing mainly with Stoicism for the minds of their citizens.

21   The 'sweet consolations for (the hardships of) life' soothe the hearts of these great nations. The phrase recurs at 6.4; Costa remarks that it 'could be the poem's motto' (Costa [1984] 51).

22-42   The achievements of Hercules are contrasted with those of Epicurus. Hercules was famously the hero of the Stoics – the great rivals of Epicureanism – and so Lucretius' mockery of the great man is not without its touch of pique. Here the mockery is in the style as much as in content: West comments on the passage that

> the famous great maw of the Nemean lion, the hydra pallisaded by its venomous snakes, the triple-chested violence of triple Geryon are all stuffed dummies, heavily padded with epic fustian. They are all harmless to us, and would be harmless even if Hercules had never dealt with them, whereas the human evils that Epicurus overcame on our behalf are still besetting us.
>
> (West [1969] 28).

22   *antistare* here means 'to outdo'. Note how the sentence begins with the key name.

23   *uera ratio* here can mean simply 'true reasoning' but the term is often used by Lucretius of Epicurean thought, allowing the poet to have this both ways: if you elevate Hercules you will stray from truth and you will also be less Epicurean (as Hercules was the Stoic hero).

24   The Nemean lion, which Hercules choked with his bare hands, was the source of his famous lion-skin costume. The style of the line shows the rationalist's attitude to these epic legends; note the ironic use of the periphrasis 'the great Nemean gaping of the lion', where the noun *hiatus* superficially means 'the roaring maw' but also has the strong sense of 'yawning' (OLD s.v. 'hio' 3c) as well as 'to mouth inarticulately' (OLD s.v. 'hio' 5).

25   The Arcadian boar was the Erymanthian boar which Hercules exhausted before catching in a net, here dismissed in the pejorative *horrens* and the deliberately inelegant final monosyllable *sus*.

26   The Cretan bull was probably that which carried Europa to Crete; the Hydra of Lerna was a poisonous snake which lived in the marshes of Lerna. When one of its many heads was cut off, several more grew in its place. The bull is named with no poetic ornament, but the Hydra is called the 'Lernaean plague with a pallisade of poisonous snakes', an

effective image using a military metaphor (*uallata*) to describe the physical threat of the monster.

28   There are two 'triple' words here to reduplicate the power of the beast; and note how Lucretius uses the epic periphrasis 'the power of Geryon' for 'strong Geryon' (cf. 4. 681, Homer, *Iliad* 23.720, Virgil, *Aeneid* 4.132). The line ends with a five-syllabled word emphasising (sardonically) the resonant name of the monster.

29-31   The text is highly unsound here, and the reading of the OCT is as good as any we are likely to get. Munro first suspected that lines 29 and 30 of the manuscript ought to be reversed and proposed that a single line had fallen out before them, even writing a 'filler' of his own to plug the gap (*quid uolucres pennis aeratis inuia stagna*).

29   The Stymphalian birds were a menace in the woods around Lake Stymphalus in Arcadia. Hercules scared them with a brass rattle and then shot some while the rest flew away.

30   Diomedes was a son of Ares and king of the Bistonians in Thrace. His four horses fed on the human flesh of his guests, and so Hercules killed Diomedes, gave his body to the horses and found that they were immediately tamed. He then took the horses back to Mycenae with him. Lucretius endows these (already frightening) beasts with fire-breathing nostrils.

31   The location is specified with three proper names in a single line: *Thracis* agrees with Diomedes, while both *Bistonias plagas* and *Ismara* are accusative with *propter* which here follows the nouns it governs. This manner of geographical placing is fully in the epic style which is here being parodied (cf., for example, Homer, *Iliad* 5. 541-5), as well as being useful in distinguishing these 'horses of Diomedes' from the other famous 'horses of Diomedes' in the Trojan War (cf. Virgil, *Aeneid* 10.581).

32-4   The serpent guarding the golden apples in the Gardens of the Hesperides was named Ladon and was shot by Hercules. Lucretius spends more time on this labour than on any of the others, lavishing three lines on the serpent and its setting. Note how the poet does not tell us who or what was 'guarding the gleaming golden apples' until the end of line 33, at the end of a tricolon crescendo of descriptive terms: *asper – acerba tuens – immani corpore serpens*. There is a nice jingle whereby the *serpens* is *seruans*.

35   The 'Atlantic shore' is here very pertinent, as it was on this labour that Hercules deceived the giant Atlas who holds up the world on his shoulders. *pelagique seuera* means 'the pitiless tracts of ocean' (M.F. Smith). The word for 'shore' (*litus*) and that for 'ocean' (*pelagi*) are juxtaposed just as the shore and the sea are next to each other in life.

36   The clinching point: these places may now be safe, but nobody goes there – not even the *barbarus*. The benefit to mankind is thus minimal if nobody would face these dangers any more. The line is ' a deliberate stylistic let-down after the inflated tone of the preceding lines' (Costa [1984] 53). The word *barbaros* in Greek means 'non-Greek'; here the term must connote 'uncivilised'.

37-8   Even if such monsters were still alive, what harm could they do us now? The imperfect subjunctive *nocerent* refers to present time. *portenta* has the sense 'prodigies', 'monsters'.

39-40   *scatit* means 'is full of'. Lucretius creates a mood of terror: note the reduplication of *trepido terrore* ('fearful fear') and also the duplication of *scatit...repleta est* followed by the trio of groves, mountains and woods, leading the reader to think that there is no escape – all to be foiled by the bathetic prosaic line 42.

42   The line and the sentence end with the key word *potestas*: we have the 'power' to avoid all these terrors.

43   Lucretius had earlier (18) urged that without a *puro pectore* the good life was impossible. Note here the alliteration of 'p'. The argument of this paragraph is that nobody but a fool would go near the sorts of place where monsters live; yet the real perils which jeopardise our happiness are with us all the time and need dealing with. The phraseology (*proelia... pericula*) is still the epic language of battles and danger, but here the danger is real. *ingratis* must agree with *nobis* – both being dative of agent after *insinuandum* meaning 'what dangers are we to find our way into whether we like it or not'.

45-8   A comprehensive list of unhelpful emotions is picked out in a series of rhetorical questions (*quantae?...quanti?...quidue?...quantas?...quid?*): desire, anxiety, fear, pride, 'filthiness', rudeness, self-indulgence, sloth. For the effects of desire, see the ending of Book 4: for the ill-effects of fear, see the prologue to Book 3. It is important here to bear in mind that Lucretius is no moralist preaching to a badly-behaved flock; as a good atomist, he believes that we are punished by our sins, and not for them – they are only bad insofar as they cause anxiety (*sollicitum*) and wreck our lives. Pride, for instance, is only bad if it prompts people to seek honours and envy those better 'placed' (cf. 3.76-8); *petulantia* is 'wantonness' or 'aggressive behaviour' which, again, is only bad if it disturbs the calm serenity of the wise man. *spurcitia* means 'sordidness' and in the immediate context probably means 'greed' (cf. Cicero, *Verrines* 2.1.94). *luxus* is clearly harmful in that it builds up unnecessary appetites for unnatural pleasures, while 'sloth' is especially bad if it prevents the reader from listening to and learning the truth (cf. 1.410-11) – the tone here is almost that of a satirist mocking the folly and vice of those around him.

45 The image in *scindunt* is violent, both 'tears open' and also 'screws' (cf. Catullus 112.2, Adams [1982] 83, 150). *acres* goes with *cuppedinis curae.*

46 The juxtaposition of *sollicitum curae* is emphatic and causal, as the *curae* cause the worry.

47-8 The sequence of questions is highly rhetorical; note that there is only one verb in the three questions which form a tricolon decrescendo as the questions get shorter. The very naming of such pejorative words as *spurcitia* is enough to indicate Lucretius' distaste, but their effects are all physical (*clades*) rather than simply 'moral' disapproval.

49 The epic language continues: these psychological enemies were 'vanquished' and then 'expelled' from the mind as if from the city by our hero.

50 Epicurus did not need the weapons (*armis*) of Hercules but could effect salvation simply by words (*dictis*).

52-3 Besides acting like a god, Epicurus also spoke about the gods with such authority that he must have been a god himself. The use of *diuinitus* is somewhat circular: he spoke 'divinely' and so he was 'divine' (emphasised by the juxtaposition of *diuinitus ipsis/ immortalibus de diuis*). Note the use of *ipsis* at the end of the line going in enjambement with the next ('the very...immortal gods'). The reference is to Epicurus' writings 'About the Gods' and 'About Holiness'.

54 The mention of *rerum naturam* rounds off the passage with a neat reference to the poem itself and leads on to the next line: Epicurus spoke about the nature of things, and 'I am following in his footsteps'. The emphasis on Epicurus' weapons being words could hardly be greater: *dictis* (50), *dare dicta* (53) and finally *dictis* (54).

195-234 'The Problem of Evil'

One key feature of Lucretius' philosophy is that the gods have no part in the making or the running of the world – which is solely the result of atomic chance. This passage is a splendid piece of reasoning on the famous 'problem of evil' whereby the world, for all its undoubted beauty, is simply too faulty to be the result of divine intelligence. The life of man is painted in colours of grim realism whereas that of animals is depicted in terms which make it sound as if animals certainly got the better of the deal when qualities were given out (a notion similar to Plato, *Protagoras* 320c-322a). The poet paints a convincing picture of the inequality between men and animals, leading one almost to the conclusion that the gods *did* construct the world – for the animals' benefit.

195-9   These lines are repeated (with minor alterations) from 2.177-81; the point is so important to Lucretius' argument that it merits repetition.

195   The sentence is to be read: *si ignorem quae sint primordia rerum* ('if I did not know what the atoms were').

196   The poet nicely contrasts the microscopic (atoms) and the telescopic (the sky) and asserts that his observation of the latter would tell him the truth even without the former. *ausim* is important: there is so much superstitious terror of the gods that it takes courage to declare that they have no place in the scheme of things (see 1. 62-79); the phrase was such a stock expression (cf. OLD s.v. 'audeo' 1c) but here we can see Lucretius restoring a vivid sense to a set phrase.

199   The defectiveness of the world is stated bluntly in four words, the last being the decisive *culpa*. Costa ([1984] 66) points out that *praeditus* is usually used of good qualities, and that therefore the phrasing here is 'edged and startling'.

200   The case for the prosecution is well structured: *principio...praeterea...tum porro.*
   Phrasing is strong: the huge *impetus* ('expanse' but also having the threatening sense of 'attack') of the sky 'roofs over' the world, calling to mind the myth of Atlas holding up the roof of the sky.

201   *auidam partem* is well chosen and emphatically positioned: the mountains are 'greedy' for territory and so they take 'the lion's share' of the land available. *ferarum* qualifies *siluae* – 'the forests (full of) wild beasts'; the verb *possedere* is stressed at the beginning of the line and end of the phrase, followed immediately by *tenent* ('they have taken and now hold').

202-3   There is a neat tricolon crescendo of: *rupes – uastaeque paludes – et mare... oras* with a slight jingle of *-te te-* in *late terrarum*. The extremes of soils are well contrasted, from rocks at one end of the spectrum to marsh at the other. The description of a sea 'which keeps the shores apart' again suggests that there is a global conspiracy to crowd humanity out of the earth's surface.

204   *duas partis* means here 'two-thirds'. The ancients believed that there were three 'zones' of the sky which cause corresponding zones of climate on earth, the torrid (equatorial) zone (*feruidus ardor*), the temperate zone, and the Arctic/Antarctic zone (*adsiduusque geli casus*). Human beings, it is argued, can only live in the temperate zone and so we are excluded from the greater part of the earth's surface. Now how the poet exaggerates the extremes of heat and cold with the (unnecessary) qualifying terms *feruidus* and then *adsiduus* in the next line.

205   Lucretius says that frost 'falls' in that it is formed in the sky and so has to drop to earth.

206-7   Even the one-third of the earth which is available is far from paradise: Lucretius points out the growth of briars which we have to remove in order to plant crops. *natura* is personified (cf. 3.931-77) and credited with her own force which our force has to counter (*sua ui...uis humana*) – making 'her' appear malicious and out to frustrate us.

208-9   *consueta* agrees with *uis humana* from line 207: note the enjambement of *ingemere* with its picture of man 'groaning over' the plough. For the nature of the 'two-toothed' mattock, see Mynors (1990) 35: it was a farm implement which needed to be strong (*ualido*) to cope with the hardness of the earth. The alliteration of 'pr' (line 210) brings out the repeated efforts required, as well as expressing the downward pressure (*pressis*) of the plough into the land as it moves forward (*pro-*).

210-12   Unlike the myth of the Golden Age when crops grew spontaneously for our food, Lucretius points out that without back-breaking effort nothing would be produced (cf. 2.1160-74), as conveyed here by the relentless use of farming terminology: the *glebas* are 'turned' by the *uomer* as we 'drill' (*subigentes*) the soil of the earth.

210   The *uomer* is the ploughshare. The 'clods' of earth are 'fertile' if we apply the right technnique to 'bring them to fruition'.

212   *liquidas in auras* is a beautiful phrase for 'into the lambent air' (M.F. Smith), the adjective *liquidas* showing both the clarity of the air and also the moisture needed for the plants to grow (see 215 below). *sponte sua* recalls the earlier emphasis on *uis* (206-7). The subject of *nequeant* must be the crops.

213-17   Even when our labours (so laboriously described at lines 206-12) prove successful, there are plenty of hazards awaiting our food-supply, from excessive sun, rain or winds. The first two lines of this passage are almost like a breathing space between the work of 206-12 and the natural disasters of 215-17.

214   The apparent total success of the farmer's efforts is evoked: 'everything' (*omnia*) throughout the lands is in leaf (*frondent*) and flower (*florent*). This is of course building up the farmer's success higher only to knock it down in the next three lines.

215-16   Earlier (204-5) we were told that two-thirds of the earth is uninhabitable because of excessive heat and cold: Lucretius now makes us realise that even the 'habitable' third is also subject to the same sudden changes which make this 'temperate zone' little better than the intemperate extremes. The repetition of *feruidus* (204) in *feruoribus* (215) and *geli*

(205) in *gelidae* (216) conveys this, as does the poet's use of plural forms (*feruoribus, pruinae*) to show that this sort of climatic disaster is no isolated occurrence but a repeated disaster.

215   The blazing heat of the sun is vivid in the juxtaposed *torret feruoribus*.

216   In contrast to the heat, the crops are now destroyed by sudden rains, the force of *subiti* being that the hapless farmer does not receive any warning and cannot take any steps to protect his livelihood.

217   The winds (note the plural for the different winds which had different names in Latin) form 'blasts' which 'disturb' the crops with a 'savage whirling'. *turbo* is properly a 'twisting' wind such as a tornado, whose force is felt in the adjective *uiolento* and the alliteration of consonantal *u*.

218-21   After the climatic disaster meted out to the crops, Lucretius turns to the animal hazards facing mankind and the threat of disease.

218-20   The subject of the verbs *alit* and *auget* is *natura*, the object being *genus ferarum*. The poet uses this word order presumably to put the beasts together in the first line enclosing 'nature', and allowing the third line of the sentence to have the question-word *cur* and the verbs together – leading to another *cur?* sentence immediately following. *horriferum* is a typical Lucretian compound adjective 'making us shudder'.

219   'Hostile to the human race': *genti* contrasts humankind with the savage *genus* of beasts; *terra marique* extends the hostility throughout the world, although the poet had already excluded the sea as an area of human habitation (203).

220   There is a petulance about *alit atque auget*; if a god had made the world he would have made it so that the world fed human beings, not so that nature fed such beasts as this. For the role of seasons and climate in disease, see 6. 1103-118 where the poet (who places the study of disease at the end of his discussion of climate and meteorology) links his ideas with those of Hippocrates' famous treatise, *Airs Waters Places*.

221   The verbs here are striking and frame the line with immense force: *adportant* is no idle metaphor – in an atomic world the seasons must 'carry' the disease-atoms. Untimely death however does not 'walk abroad' except in a metaphorical sense, although the plague section of Book 6 (esp. 6.1090-102) makes it clear Lucretius understood that disease is spread through the air. Mention here of 'untimely death' leads to the picture of the wailing child.

222-7   These are among the best-remembered lines of the poem. The passage combines a neat simile (the newborn child like a sailor thrown out of the waves) with hard realism about the process of birth.

98

222   The waves are *saeuis* (picking up the theme of savagery from 218-19).

223-4   The child is like a sailor – very much like Odysseus in fact who was
        famously cast on the shore of Scheria naked (Homer, *Odyssey* 5-6) –
        only this 'sailor' is cast into the 'shores of light' rather than the shores
        of land. *infans* properly means 'unable to speak'. There is a neat jingle
        whereby the *nauita* needs *uitali* help, and in the enjambement of *indigus
        omni* (in need of all)/ *uitali auxilio* (assistance to live).

225   The process of giving birth is not romanticised: we have the 'pushings'
        (*nixibus* cf. OLD s.v. 'nixus' b) from the womb (*aluo*) by which nature
        'has spilt' the child out – a liquid image all too appropriate to the context.

226-7   The infant wails with a lot of 'u' sounds: the poet then adds the sardonic
        point that the child might well cry in view of the misery ahead of him
        in his life.

228-34 The passage ends with a short piece idealising the life of beasts who
        need no childcare, clothes or walls to protect them. This is simply
        concluding the argument that the world was not made by the gods with
        people in mind – as the evidence suggests that beasts come off better in
        the global economy than we do.

228   The beasts are *uariae* by nature, whereas humans merely seek *uarias*
        clothes (231). The array of animals is well brought out by the list of
        pecudes armenta feraeque – flocks, herds and wild animals.

229   *crepitacillis* are babies' rattles.

230   The poet pokes gentle fun at the way in which the 'feeding nurse' has
        to coax the infant with 'broken' words; Costa ([1984] 68) points out that
        infractus means 'mincing' or 'effeminate'.

231   Humans have to change their clothes to suit the heat or cold of the
        season, whereas animals wear the same skins all year round.

232-4   The passage ends on an idyllic note as the pacific life of the beasts, fed
        to surfeit by nature, is contrasted with that of the weary human farmer.
        The irony here is that we artificially 'spoil' our children with our
        ridiculous baby-talk coaxing them to eat and finding them clothes to
        wear, whereas animals are really 'spoilt' by the wealth of nature and
        their own strength and independence. Animals do not own property and
        so 'do not need weapons and high walls to protect what is their own',
        since they all own everything in common and crime is therefore non-
        existent – a notion found also in Aristophanes' *Ecclesiazusai* where the
        women of Athens arrange a similar communist system.

233-4   Note the largesse of earth herself and nature the 'fashioner of things'
        who supplies 'all things to all' (*omnibus omnia*) generously.

Book Six

The Plague at Athens

The question of the ending of the poem is one of the most vexed in classical scholarship, as Lucretius concludes his poem with a dark and depressing picture of the plague which beset Athens in 430 BC; many of the details of Lucretius' account are derived from Thucydides, *History of the Peloponnesian War* 2.47-52. One wonders why a poet who tells us that we can live a life worthy of the gods, and who began his text with a paean of joy at the creativity of Venus, should leave his readers with this bleak and nihilistic threnody.

Some have seen it as Patin's famous '*Anti-Lucrèce chez Lucrèce*', whereby the poet who claimed to be irreligious and glad to be so could not disguise the 'true' melancholic despair which comes out in passages such as this one. The theory is only worth discussing if it makes us realise that Lucretius' brand of optimism is no pious fantasy but is rooted in his knowledge of the real world, warts, plagues and all. Epicurus himself died in agony (Diogenes Laertius 10.15) and yet died happy, death is after all 'nothing to us' (3.830), and the poet can make the reader look even at this spectacle of death without losing his sense of wonder and his need to understand.

Others have taken more extreme views of the epilogue. Minyard ([1985] 60-1) sees it as a form of mockery of the Athenian city-state looking forward to the birth of Epicurus who would save it – although there is nothing in the text to support this reading. This 'political' reading would turn the epilogue into allegory of the death of the political state and leave the puzzled reader to deduce this: above all, Lucretius is never slow to draw moral conclusions and yet the 'before and after' point relating Athens of 430 BC to the Athens of Epicurus (with which the book began) is not made clear. Furthermore, the plague did not (in fact) bring political life to a grinding halt – and neither did Epicurus do anything for the political life of his city.

The theory is not perhaps wholly without merit: Book 5 showed us the growth of civilisation and its superficial nature as a recent development which still leaves mankind racked with 'primitive' fear and superstition. Lucretius is concerned neither to sentimentalise primitivism nor to praise progress, but simply to argue that material progress by itself is no use without listening to Epicurus. Seen in these terms, the plague is an extreme example of the way that life can force everyone to suffer and it shows the futility of relying on health and wealth (or the gods) for our happiness. The plague might also be seen as a moral allegory of our need for Epicurus' teaching in facing death and a historical case-study of the way in which society breaks down under the pressure of suffering.

This is perhaps to go too far. The allegory is not pointed out and the whole thrust of the passage is that nobody – not even the most pious Epicurean – would have escaped this plague. There is no distinction drawn between good death and bad death, and the squabbling selfishness of the survivors shows us the moral effects of sickness on human society. The plague was an extraordinary event to end a book full of extraordinary things, and the epilogue affords insight into the plight of the sick and compassion for their pain together with another opportunity to ram the anti-theological point firmly home as the poet insists that the gods gave no help – except that people turned their temples into impromptu hospitals for the sick.

Finally, there is the aesthetic and artistic dimension to be evaluated. Lucretius often ends his books with a picture of the 'sick' or the wretched (the dying in Books 3 and 6, the lovers in Book 4, the plangent ploughman in Book 2); and this is no mere *Schadenfreude* but rather a demonstration that for him these atomic scientific principles *matter* because they relate to real human beings. While the Epicurean may choose to live in his Garden, he does not have to be an ivory-tower recluse; his philosophy brings him face to face with the imperfection of the world (5. 195-234 above) and its inhabitants, and there would be less reason to seek out the serenity of the garden if the world around were not so harsh. The ending of the book is in some ways a 'test' for the reader who will thus be able to see for himself whether his conversion to Epicureanism can withstand these pages of despair. More importantly, it is a demonstration of the need for Epicurus' teaching and the way in which the study of nature can find fascination and meaning in this account of meaningless suffering. The passage has a tragic dimension, leaving us rather as we are at the end of plays such as Euripides' *Trojan Women*, faced with human beings destroyed mentally and physically, often without deserving such suffering (see Penwill on this point). The medium here is, in some ways, the message: the aesthetic contemplation even of extreme suffering is the only ultimate source of pleasure (and therefore happiness) in a world which (like ourselves) is doomed to death and oblivion. Wisdom may bring happiness, but that wisdom requires us to accept the tragedy of life and death and still remain content – even in the knowledge of our imminent and painful death. No facile optimism could do justice to the ending of this great work; there is ring-composition in the sense that the poem begins with birth and ends with death, and the reader is thus invited by this bleak ending to take up Book 1 and start all over again.

1138-40 The sequence of words moves from the general principles and theory (*ratio*) to the increasingly specific *aestus* (current of infected air), the defined area (Athens), the precise details of fields, roads and finally the city itself.

1138 *morborum et mortifer* describes the sequence of disease and then death, as in 1144. *aestus* had been used only at 1056 of the electric current from the magnet; it has not been used of the force of the disease, but well conveys the sense of the *morbida uis* in motion.

1139 *Cecropis* adds an epic touch in alluding to the first recorded king of Athens (Cecrops), although the events which Lucretius is going to describe actually took place much later. The epic tone continues with the tricolon of verbal phrases with effects such as the 'fields of death' (*funestos...agros*) – when fields are usually associated with growth of new crops – the alliterative *uastauitque uias* which shows us that this enemy is ravaging the streets of their people, and finally the telling metaphor *exhausit*, letting us see the plague 'drink dry' the city of its citizens.

1141 Thucydides (2.48) states that the plague is said to have arisen in 'Ethiopia in Upper Egypt', before going on to Egypt and then to Libya and much of 'the territory of the King of Persia'.

1142 The long journey of the plague is aptly conveyed by the string of participles (*ueniens – ortus – permensus*) and the very length of the description of the journey, complete with the epic language of 'the swimming plains' (cf. 405, 5.488).

1143 After the long string of participles, the main verb *incubuit* at the beginning of the line (strengthened further by *tandem* which follows it) has tremendous power, and after the sequence of 'travelling' words the verb evokes a sudden stop. Pandion was a king of Athens and father of Procne and Philomela. The name also suggests the Greek word *pan* ('all', everything') to chime neatly with the Latin word *omni* next to it. Again how Lucretius emphasises that the plague attacked not property but people – and the whole people at that, not just a few.

1144 *dabantur* suggests the handing over of human sacrifices to an evil monster, such as happened in the mythological case of the Minotaur (see Catullus 64.76). *cateruatim* is a strong way of stressing the numbers dying; for the form of the adverb, cf. *aceruatim* at 1263. Lucretius' older contemporary Sisenna was fond of such formations, as we are told by Gellius (12.15).

1145-50 The first stage of the sickness. Thucydides' account reads as follows:

> First there were violent burnings in the head and reddening and inflammation of the eyes seized them: inside the head the throat and the tongue began at once to bleed and the breath came out unnatural and foul.   (2.49.2)

It will be clear that Lucretius has added several details of his own (for example the 'black' throat 'sweating'), and in particular the condition of the voice and tongue is given in more detail. The foul breath is left until later (1154-5).

1146 *duplicis* is perhaps an unnecessary detail (Thucydides merely says 'eyes'). Note the use of the words *luce suffusa* for the inflammation: *suffundo* commonly means 'to cause a liquid to well up to the surface (esp. blood)' (OLD s.v. 'suffundo' 2), and *lux* has the meaning 'eyesight' as well as the primary meaning 'light' or (here) 'glow'. The phrase thus connotes eyes glowing underneath with a welling of blood, the colour being brought out in *rubentes* with which the line and sentence end.

1147-9 Note the enjambement of *atrae/ sanguine* and the double surprise that this blood is not only black but is a form of sweat. Lucretius also glosses the anatomical terms with descriptive phrases almost in the manner of Homeric formulae: the throat is thus the 'path of the voice', the tongue is the 'interpreter of the mind' – a poetic colouring quite foreign to the prose of Thucydides. Lucretius varies the vocabulary so that *sudabat* of the throat becomes *manabat* of the tongue, *sanguine* becomes *cruore*. Line 1150 is a brilliant example of a tricolon in triple chiasmus: the adjectives/participles (A) are arranged with their qualifying ablative nouns (B) in the sequence ABBAAB, thus:

debilitata malis/ motu grauis/ aspera tactu.

1151-9 The second stage of the sickness; Thucydides' account reads:

> Then sneezing and hoarseness came upon them, and soon after the disease descended to the chest accompanied by a violent cough. When it passed into the stomach it churned it up and all the eructations of bile that have ever been named by the doctors came up, accompanied by great pain.   (2. 49.3)

1151 Lucretius has just described the effects of the plague on the throat: now he passes down the body to the chest and the *cor*, the movement stressed by the pair of *con-* verbs. The meaning of *ubi* with the pluperfect tense is 'whenever' and the sense here is 'when in each case...'.

1152 *cor* means 'heart' (and the qualifying adjective *maestum* would support this) and Thucydides uses the Greek word *kardia*, which also usually means 'heart' but in this context must mean 'stomach' (see Rusten *ad loc.*). It is tempting to argue that Lucretius has simply mistranslated the Greek word and yet his common sense has not allowed him to ascribe to the heart the symptoms of vomiting etc., which Thucydides ascribes to this stage of the sickness. (See Commager 105-7, 114-15.)

103

1153 An effective metaphor, 'the bolts of life', refers to the 'interlocking union of soul and body atoms on which life depended'. (Brown on 1.415).

1154-5 It may seem a retrograde step, after Lucretius has descended from the head to the chest, to go back up to the breath from the mouth: and Thucydides (as we have seen) had kept the foul breath with the head. It does fit well enough here, however, as the breath leaving the body is almost a synonym for death (see OLD s.v. 'spiritus' 2b, 4a) and thus prepares the reader for the simile of the corpses in the next line.

1155 The rotting corpses appear again later on in the book (1215ff.). Here they are brought in partly as a vivid simile for the rancid smell of the sick man's breath, partly to reinforce the theme of death which pervades the whole section.

1156 Note the effective juxtaposition of *totius omne*. The MS of this line reads simply: *atque animi prorsum uires totius omne* and a word has clearly dropped out. A later MS adds *et* before *omne*, but a better reading is Wakefield's conjecture that *tum* has been lost before *uires* – a plausible explanation as the scribe will have seen *prorsum* and omitted *tum* because he thought he had already written it, a common cause of manuscript error.

1157 For the phrase *leti limine* see 2.960, 5.373-5, where Costa cites the Greek parallels at Homer, *Iliad* 5.646, *Odyssey* 14.156, Aeschylus, *Agamemnon* 1291. It is interesting to see how this rationalist poet – who has (in Book 3 especially) dispelled all belief in myth and superstition – should now 'remythologise' the world in his choice of poetic phrasing. (On this topic see Gale *passim*.)

1158-9 Note the expressive assonance of *anxius angor assidue*; for the idea of personified anxiety as companion, see Horace, *Odes* 3.1.37-40. The poet mixes the physical and the mental suffering verbally in expressing how the one brings the other in its wake: *malis* is physical pain, *angor* is mental distress; *gemitus* is a groan of pain, while *querella* is a lament of grief.

1160-2 Thucydides' account reads:

> Most people were then stricken with an empty retching which caused violent spasms. Some people found that this symptom stopped at this stage, others only much later.   (2.49.4)

Lucretius omits the detail of the retching being ineffectual but adds the lengthy and exhausting nature of the symptoms.

1161 *nerui* are properly the sinews or 'tendons' of the body, and *corripere* must be taken with it; the image created by the phrasing is of pulling the sinews like draw-strings through a purse, thus causing the body to twitch and double up. The word *corripere* is used several times by Lucretius to mean 'arouse' 'wake up' (3.925, 4.999) and is thus ideal here to evoke the constant waking up of sick people in need of sleep – which causes yet more fatigue.

1163-77 The heat of the disease. The patients are not externally hot to the touch but they burn with a feverish inner fire. Thucydides' account reads:

> The outside of the body was not too hot to touch, and there was no paleness either, the skin being rather red and livid with little ulcers breaking out on it. Inside the body however there was a feverish burning such that people could not stand the touch even of the lightest clothing but rather wanted to be totally naked – or best of all to dive into cold water. Many of the sufferers who had nobody to care for them did just that, jumping into the water storage-tanks to relieve their unquenchable thirst which did not change whether they drank much or little. (2.49.5)

1164 The phrasing *corporis in summo summam partem* stresses the 'most outside part of the outside of the body'. This topmost surface is contrasted with *intima pars* at 1168 below. Note the polyptoton of *summo summam*.

1166 The simile *quasi inustis* is not found in Thucydides, who speaks of the ulcers 'flowering' on the skin. Lucretius perhaps felt that the flower metaphor was too cheerful and substituted his own more pained comparison with the branding of slaves and criminals.

1167 The *sacer ignis* is erysipelas: the phrasing reminds the reader of the Greek *hiera nosos* ('sacred disease'), the superstitious term for epilepsy which Hippocrates discussed in his influential essay 'On the Sacred Disease'. Lucretius clearly shares Hippocrates' anti-theological view of sickness.

1168-9 The fire is vividly conveyed by the epanalepsis of *flagrabat...flagrabat* and the striking alliteration of *f* as the fire blazes. The bones often feel cold and heat in epic poetry (e.g. Virgil, *Aeneid* 2.120). The simile of the furnace is, again, something which Lucretius has added to Thucydides' account.

1170 *posses* is addressed to the reader ('you could...'), although the events described are no longer in fact available for examination.

1171 The phrasing is vague, as the poet does not tell us that he is thinking of clothes but leaving us to infer it, perhaps in order to evoke the incoherent discomfort of the sufferers who do not know what they need. The phrase *uentum et frigora semper* is blunt and crude in expression, and *uertere in utilitatem* sounds prosaic.

1172-3 Note the oxymoron of *gelidos ardentia* and the chiasmus of *fluuios – membra – corpus – in undas*. We already know that the body is on fire with the sickness (1168-9) and the phrase *ardentia morbo* is to emphasise the point further by contrast with the cold of *frigora...gelidos*. Similarly 1170 has shown us the sick unable to bear clothes, and *nudum* here picks up this point.

1173-4 Notice the intensifying of *membra dabant* into *praecipites...inciderunt*.

1174 Some manuscripts read *nymphis*, and it has been argued that this reading is correct as the nymphs are associated by metonymy with the waters themselves (cf. OLD s.v. 'nympha' 1b). The obvious emendation is to *lymphis* which is clearer, if less poetic.

1174-5 The falling is stressed with the concatenation of the three words *praecipites...alte/ inciderunt*.

1175 The thirst of the sick causes the grotesque picture here of them diving into the water with mouths agape, a point which the following lines will amplify. *ipso* emphasises the part of the body in question, as at 1207, 4.1044.

1176 The length of the adverb *insedabiliter* is expressive of the interminable drinking (cf. *insatiabiliter* at 978, 3.907). Note also the paradoxes of the 'dry' thirst 'drenching' their bodies, making the great small (*multum paruis* in oxymoronic juxtaposition), the single 'rainstorm' (*imbrem* – presumably meaning the containers full of rain-water) made into a set of separate 'drops'.

1178 For *requies*, cf. Thucydides 2.49.6: 'throughout all this they could find no means of rest and they could not sleep'. Lucretius unpacks the generality of *nec requies erat* into the more specific and simple *defessa iacebant corpora*, and returns to their insomnia in 1181.

1179 The inability of the doctors to do anything is mentioned also in Thucydides ('at first the doctors were incapable of treating the disease because of their ignorance', 2.47.4). Lucretius does not include Thucydides' further point that in fact doctors suffered from plague more than other groups because of their more frequent contact with it. It might be argued that *mussabat* hints at this with the implication that the doctor 'mutters' because he is unwilling to breathe the air and speak clearly; but it is equally possible that the muttering is the result of puzzlement and that he has 'silenced his fear' (*tacito...timore*) to see the patient in the first place. The alliteration of *m* and the juxtaposition of *mussabat tacito* suggest faint speech blending into silence.

1180-1 The poet lingers on the eyes of the sick man with three descriptive phrases (with no connective to join them) to bring out the pathos and the pain. The eyes are 'wide open' (*patentia*), 'burning with disease' (*ardentia morbis*), and 'knowing no sleep' (*expertia somno*). The phrase *totiens...uersarent* evokes the constant rolling of the eyeballs – a symptom not mentioned by Thucydides. The periphrasis *lumina...oculorum* is not mere decoration: *lumen* means 'a source of light', often a lamp, which gives *ardentia* ('burning') more point. The poet adds *oculorum* to make the meaning of *lumina* unambiguous here.

1182-96 The approach of death: a passage drawn not from Thucydides but rather from the writings of the school of Hippocrates. Lucretius' style in this passage is very close to that of Hippocrates' *Epidemics* in its stark recital of symptoms – without connecting words – and its reference (1197-8) to the days on which symptoms occurred.

1182 *signa* has the philosophical sense of 'evidence from which to infer the unseen' and also 'symptoms of sickness'.

1183-4 The mental effects of the disease. Hippocrates had noted the incidence of madness in patients who were extremely ill (*Epidemics* 1.12) and the Greeks often linked the symptoms of disease with the phenomenon of madness, most obviously in the epileptic fit (frothing mouth and rolling eyes) seen for instance in the case of Heracles (Euripides, *Heracles* 868, 932-4: cf. *Bacchae* 1122-3, *Medea* 1173-5, Hippocrates *On the Sacred Disease* 7). Lucretius details the mental disturbance in terms of the inner state of mind, then in terms of physical symptoms observable by anybody (the gloomy brow). He then passes imperceptibly into internal physical symptoms only known to the sufferer (the ringing in the 'troubled' ears – *sollicitae* is usually a 'mental' word) and then again symptoms observable by anybody (irregular breathing). 1184 has an effective clash of *triste* (sad) and *furiosus* (mad), evoking the manic oscillation between depression and anger in the victim.

1186 Irregular breathing is well suggested by an unusual metrical break at the end of the second foot to leave the short panting breath isolated, followed by the long slower phrase for the slow breath.

1187f Lucretius does not merely mention the wetness of the perspiration (*madens*) but *sees* it 'gleaming' (*splendidus*) on the neck; note also the epic way in which the colour and the taste of the spittle is conveyed, complete with alliteration of *c* and assonance of *u – a* in *sputa minuta*. The phrase *croci contacta colore* makes the spittle like some fine cloth 'dyed with saffron', a surprisingly elevated and beautiful term for the grotesque subject.

1190   For *nerui*, see 1161. Notice the chiasmus of *nerui trahere – tremere artus*.

1191-2   Description of the slow upward progress of coldness will remind the reader of the death of Socrates, whose hemlock similarly affected the extremities and then rose towards the torso (Plato, *Phaedo* 117e-118e; but cf. Gill (1973) for doubts about the physiology of this). Lucretius evokes the relentless slow surge of coldness both in the enjambement and in the lengthy adverb *minutatim*.

1193-4   Note the juxtaposition of *nares nasi* and the jingle of *cauati...caua*. The word *frigora* picks up *frigus* from 1191, and the whole passage is a study in the shrinking and compressing effects of cold, the eyes and temples sinking in because the skin shrinks against the skull, the coldness also making the skin hard, so that the end-result of being *frigida* is being *rigida* in line 1196.

1195   This line is a famous textual crux. The manuscript reads *duraque inhoretiacetrectumfrons tentamebat*, and most editors rely on the fourth-century grammarian and lexicographer Nonius Marcellus who appears to quote an improved version of the line as: *duraque in ore iacens rictu frons tenta manebat*. Better sense is rendered by Richter's ingenious suggestion of: *duraque in archiatri tactum; frons tenta tumebat*, reading the rare word *archiater* ('chief physician') which is found only in inscriptions and which a scribe unfamiliar with it would have 'corrected'. The difficulty with this reading is metrical: the initial 'i' of the Greek word *iatros* being long, it is difficult to see how the Latinised version of the Greek word could suddenly have a short 'i', and scanning the word as three syllables (*archjatri*) is also dubious. However, faced with either this or the nonsense in the MS, I have printed Richter's suggestion *faute de mieux*.

1196   *rigida* reminds us of *frigida* earlier on. The epithet is transferred from the limbs which are stiff to the death which causes this.

1197-8   Thucydides asserts that: 'most people died on the eighth or the sixth day' (2.49.6). Note here the epic variation of *lumine solis* to *lampade* and the fine phrase *reddere uitam* ('gave up their life'; see OLD s.v. 'reddere' 11a), with the sense of life being returned as if on loan (for which idea, cf. 3.971 above) and also 'rendering an account'.

1199-   The alternatives to a quick death were hardly preferable. Thucydides'
1214   account is thus:

> But if people survived this, then the disease went down to the bowels and caused severe ulcers and a flood of diarrhoea, causing most of them to die later on from the weakness brought on by this. The disease first fixed in the head and then sickened every part of

the body one after another. Even if they escaped the worst effects, the disease still seized their extremities and left its mark on them: it assailed their genitals, the tips of their hands and feet, and many people only survived when they lost these parts – and some lost eyes in this way. Total amnesia also seized some as soon as they began to recover and they recognised neither themselves nor their friends. (2. 49.7-8)

1199 *funera leti* sounds tautologous: the effect is both emphatic and sombre.

1200 Notice the chiastic arrrangement of nouns and adjectives, with *taetris...nigra* juxtaposed for effect. *proluuie alui* has a sonorous sound.

1201 *tabes letumque* is a nice example of *hysteron proteron* in that it looks as though the words are back to front, since decay usually follows death – the effect here, as often, is to highlight that the decay is caused by death.

1202-4 Thucydides says nothing of the headache and nosebleed; the addition of the nosebleed makes an effective antithesis to the flood of diarrhoea, the phrasing being reminiscent of Nicander, *Theriaca* 301 ('blood wells up through the nostrils, throat and ears...', describing the attack of the 'blood-letting snake').

In the present passage note the frothing double 'r' sound in *corruptus*, the hissing 's' alliteration and the emphatic single verb *ibat* as the elaborately described blood simply pours out.

1204 *corpus* cannot be translated as 'body' here but refers rather to the man's whole strength and 'substance' (M.F. Smith). The line states that the man's strength ebbed away with his blood and so it was as if his body were passing away.

1205 Note the continuation of ideas: *fluebat* moves straight into the noun *profluuium,* the blood is now *taeter* (disgusting), picking up *corruptus* (tainted) from line 1203, and *exierat* applies to the patient who 'escapes' danger but also reminds us of the blood 'issuing forth' (*ibat* 1203). *acre* is a good choice of word here; it means 'sharp' or 'pungent' referring to the smell of the blood, and also describes the violent action of the outpouring of the blood.

1206 *neruos et artus* is a general description of 'sinews and limbs', about to be made gruesomely specific with *partes genitales*, made climactic by the final word *ipsas*. For the euphemism of 'genital parts', see 4.1044.

1208 The poet continues the horror. Some people, in dread of death, castrated themselves or lived deprived of limbs. The passive participle *priuati* (parallel to Thucydides' participle *steriskomenoi*, although Thucydides may only mean that these men no longer had the use of these parts rather than drastic removal) leaves open the possibility that the castration was performed either by the patient himself or by the doctor. It is noteworthy that the poet chooses here to use the epic phrase *limina leti* ('threshold of death') and have 'death' back to back with 'life', as line 1208 ends with *leti* while 1209 begins with *uiuebant*. Note also the effective alliteration of *limina leti* and *priuati parte.*

1210   The poet plays with the words in a neat chiastic arrangement: they were without *manibus* but they still *manebant* in life, just as in the previous line they *uiuebant* without their *uirili* part. The enjambement of *uiuebant/ in uita* well evokes the prolonged life of the mutilated patient.

1211   The use of *lumina* is a pun: the surface meaning is simply that the patient went blind; but the term also means 'the light of life' (OLD s.v. 'lumen' 3) and so we have the paradox that they kept the *lumen* by losing their *lumina.*

1212   The line picks up the theme of fear of death from line 1208 and rounds off the sentence with effective closure, emphasised by the alliteration of *mortis metus* and the final adjective *acer* (to be used of the smell of death, line 1217). The fear of death is of course one of the ethical concerns in the poem, and yet it is unlikely that Lucretius is here mocking the unfortunate sufferers who made a rational choice between mutilation and annihilation: this differs totally from the neurotic wretches in 3.31-90, whose fear of death ruins their lives.

1213-14 Amnesia and confusion are also mentioned by Thucydides (see above note on 1199-1214). The totality of the forgetfulness is brought out by the enjambement throwing *cunctarum* into emphasis. *ipsi* is also something of a surprise: the sufferers lost their memory and could not recognise *...themselves.* We might expect them to forget friends or acquaintainces, but the poet endows them with the worst possible form of amnesia.

1215-24 Lucretius has been describing humans sufferering from plague, and he returns to this in line 1225. In this interlude he turns to animals. The relevant passage in Thucydides reads as follows:

> Though there were many dead bodies lying about unburied, the birds and animals that eat human flesh either did not come near them, or, if they did taste the flesh, died of it afterwards. Evidence of this may be found in the fact that there was a complete disappearance of all birds of prey: they were not to be seen either round the bodies or anywhere else. But dogs, being domestic animals, provided the best opportunity of observing this effect of the plague.
>
> (2.50.1-2)

What strikes the reader at once is the manner in which Lucretius has turned the material into epic verse with the grandiose phrasing such as the 'race of winged creatures', the 'sad generations of wild beasts' and the 'trusty power of dogs', as well as the unusually effective phrase *illis solibus* for 'in those days'. Lucretius also imparts a power to his poetry by adding to Thucydides such features as the *sad* wild beasts not coming out of the woods, and the plucky dogs refusing to give up without a struggle. Thucydides uses the dogs as good scientific evidence as they were readily observable, whereas Lucretius invests the animals with real pathos: they are trusty (unlike the human beings of 1239ff) and show more courage and determination than some hopeless humans (1229ff).

1215 The jingle of *humi...inhumata* strongly suggests that corpses ought to be buried and not left on top of the ground, while the verbal reduplication (stressed by enjambement) of *corpora.../ corporibus* depicts the physical piling up of the corpses.

1216 The epic periphrasis with *genus* can be traced back through Ennius (e.g. *Annales* 10, 81) to Homer (e.g. *Iliad* 9.130, *Odyssey* 8.481, 7.206). The effect of this raising of the register of language is twofold: it creates a tension between the disease and degradation of the animals and the elevated language in which it is described, and it also links the present passage with the opening of Homer's *Iliad* where a plague hits the Greek camp (and where dogs are among the first to suffer).

1217-18 Notice the chiasmus here in the contrast of *procul absiliebat...languebat... propinqua*, and the inexorable manner in which the immediacy of death is brought out by the verb *gustarat* ('tasted') leading with no hesitation to *languebat morte*. The smell of death is *acer*, as was the fear of death in line 1212; as in all good Epicurean philosophy, the senses are the primary sources of information.

1219 *solibus illis* is similar to 1197, Virgil, *Eclogue* 9.52, *Aeneid* 3.203 and can be read as simply variation for *illo tempore* or some such. The term is highly effective, carrying the sense of the oppressive heat of the sun, unwelcome to animals even in the best of health (cf. Virgil, *Eclogue* 2.8-13), and possibly acting as a contributory cause of suffering and even of the outbreak of disease in the first place. Most obviously it is a touch of psychological realism, in that one of the chief symptoms of the plague was a burning fever (1168ff) which would feel like intolerable heat in the middle of summer. As often, Lucretius takes what appears to be a cliché and invests it with life and vigour.

1220 Lucretius is fond of the periphrasis *saecla* + genitive, using it 44 times in the poem. The adjective *tristia* is perfect, adding pathos to the account of beasts refusing to leave the forests.

1221-2   The immediacy of effect is sharp in the assonant phrase *morbo et morie-bantur*, as the sick became the dead with rapidity and are despatched with a peremptory phrase. Note also the repetition of *languebant* from line 1218.

1222   'The trusty power of dogs' is an epic phrase: cf. 4.681, Virgil, *Aeneid* 4.132. The poet's use of the monosyllable *uis* at the end of the line renders the rhythm of the hexameter bumpy and uneven – a device used by later poets to describe the comic (5.25, Virgil, *Georgics* 1.181), the pompous (Virgil, *Aeneid* 1.65) or the ox crashing to the ground at Virgil, *Aeneid* 5.481. Lucretius uses the device more than later poets, and it clearly has less onomatopoeic force for him than it did for them; its effect here is to stress the word *canum*, which is forced to carry its usual speech accent on the first syllable and also a metrical ictus on the second. The epic phrase also brings out the 'power' of the dogs – a power which will be tested to the limit and beyond in the succeeding lines by the power of the disease (*uis morbida*).

1223   The word *strata* commonly means of 'paved streets' from the verb *sterno*, deriving from the laying of paving stones down on the earth. The juxtaposition of *strata uiis* is clearly deliberate, leaving a strong image in the reader's mind of the dogs laid out on the roads like slabs of pavement. *animam ponebat* is a grand pathetic phrase to use of dumb animals; and *aegre* is another pun, as the primary meaning of *aeger* is 'sick' while the adverb generally means 'with difficulty'. The dogs give up their life with a struggle (*aegre*) but also in a sickly manner.

1224   The line is full of epic rhetorical and poetic effects. The strong alliteration and assonance of *extorquebat enim uitam uis morbida membris*; the planting of the tiny word *uis* in the middle of the phrase expressive of the tiny but invincible power of this invisible sickness; the violence of the metaphor *extorquebat* and the resounding end-stopped quality of the line, as final and chilling as a death-sentence. If line 1223 suggested that the dogs 'laid down their lives', this line sets the record straight by showing us how the force of the disease 'wrung' the life out of their limbs.

1225   Lucretius now returns to human beings. The line is framed by two words expressive of the 'loneliness' of the funerals: the first is pathetically specific ('unaccompanied') while the second has a wide range of emotional significance, meaning 'desolate' 'dreary' and also 'huge' (once again drawing our attention to the great numbers of dead). The adjective *uasta* sets up a nice paradox between the sense of desolation and the 'crowding' implicit in *certabant*.

1226-9 This is a new point: what cured some killed others, and so there was no reliable medical treatment. The argument reminds us of the modes of Scepticism (see 4.469-521, Annas and Barnes *passim*). The link with what has just preceded is more verbal echo than any link of sense: *communis* picks up from *incomitata* and *certa* from *certabant*.

1227-9 *quod* here means 'that which' and is the subject of *dederat* – what had given to one person (*ali*) the ability to live ('to roll the life-giving breezes of air in his mouth') was *exitio* (predicative dative, 'cause of death') to others (*aliis*). Notice here the almost humorous contrast between life – expressed in long lavish periphrases – and the short sharp shock of sudden death (*exitio letumque*). This well evokes the difference between the prolonged enjoyment of life and the suddenness of annihilation; the phrasing is also psychologically subtle: after life-threatening illness even such 'ordinary' things as breathing and seeing the sky become something to savour and enjoy, so that the air becomes the 'life-giving breezes of air', the sky is the 'temples of the heavens' and the breath is 'rolled' around the mouth like wine.

1230-51 Some mental and social effects of the plague.

1230-4 The despair of the infected man (cf. Thucydides 2.51.4):

> the most fearful part of all was the despair into which people fell when they realised that they had caught the disease – for they at once gave themselves up to utter hopelessness and refused to fight the disease.

Note how Lucretius changes 'most fearful' (*deinotaton*) into 'most wretched' (*miserandum...aerumnabile*) and how he charges the passage with a deep sympathy beyond the recitation of the medical facts.

1232 The metaphor of *implicitum* is that of being caught in a net – a metaphor with a long literary pedigree and most famously used by Aeschylus, *Agamemnon* (1127, with Fraenkel's note). For its use here, cf. 4.1149 (of being entangled in the net of Venus) and Commager 113. The juxtaposition of *morbo morti* underlines the assumption in the sufferer's mind of the inevitability of death, further enhanced by the phrasing *damnatus ut esset*. The *ut* is more likely to mean 'on the grounds that' rather than 'as if'.

1233-4 Note the pity in these lines: the 'sad' heart as he 'lay losing his spirit'; the asyndeton between *iacebat* and *amittebat* is effective in making 1234 a parallel restatement of 1233 and emphasising it; the assonance of *animam amittebat*; and above all the brilliant touch of *funera respectans* as the sufferer becomes increasingly depressed as he 'gazes on funerals/deaths', a psychological detail not found in Thucydides. *ibidem* suggests that the sufferer died 'where he lay' – the effort of moving being well beyond him by this stage.

1235   Thucydides gave two aspects of the 'most fearful thing of all', the despair of the sick and the unavoidable contagion of the sickness. Lucretius joins these two together through the twin sense of *funera respectans*: in his despair he is 'looking only on death', but he is also 'gazing on funerals' – and there were plenty of funerals to gaze upon as the disease was so infectious.

1236   The disease is personified as 'greedy', never ceasing to 'acquire' (*apisci*). The contagion from one to another is reflected in the juxtaposition of *aliis alios*.

1237   The animals are brought in as both a parallel and a simile: the disease spread among people just as it did among animals – and (Lucretius implies) the people died like animals, just as Thucydides described them dying 'like sheep' (2.51.4). Lucretius amplifies the simile with the epic compound adjective *lanigeras* and the epic periphrasis *bucera saecla*, which is a Greek term (from *boukeros* 'ox-horned') joined to a Latin term *saecla* (see above 1220). The whole phrase is repeated from 2.661-2 and also 5.866; the point of the phrasing here is presumably to stress the distinction between the 'low' degradation of the death and the 'high' style of the description.

1238-46 Thucydides' account reads:

> When people refused to go near each other out of fear, they died all alone and many households were emptied completely with the shortage of anyone to look after them; if on the other hand they did approach the sick they died, especially those who made a claim to be good people – they did not spare themselves out of shame, but went to see their friends – I mention this since by the end even the members of their own households tired of making the laments over the dying, overcome by the magnitude of their own misfortune.   (2.51.5)

1238   Note the verbal accumulation in the polyptoton of *funere funus* well evoking the physical piling of the bodies (cf. 3.71).

1239   There is a slight oxymoron in *fugitabant uisere*, the first word suggesting flight while the second suggests movement *towards*.

1240   Greed for life and fear of death are, for Lucretius, two sides of the same coin: see, for example, 3.59-64 and notice here the triad of greed – death – fear.

1241-2 Lucretius is here at his most censorious as the personified force of *Incuria* ('neglect') enters like a *deus ex machina* and exacts a punishment from those who neglect their own. The appropriateness of the punishment reminds the reader of the *Litai* passage in Homer, *Iliad* 9. 502-14, where those who do not accept an apology are themselves made the guilty ones whom the personified 'Prayers' drive to commit acts of madness. Likewise here the neglectful are themselves neglected and die alone soon in disgrace (*turpi*) and suffering (*mala*). The word *mactans* is effective, suggesting the ritual sacrifice performed by this god *Incuria* in bringing about the death of the wicked man; note also the lingering over the suffering of the wicked in the catalogue of *desertos opis expertis*. For this sort of allegorical personification (*prosopopoeia*) compare the figure of Nature in 3.931-951 and also the talking Laws in Plato's *Crito* 50a.

1243 *ibant* here means 'died', but again there is a slight paradox in that these are the ones who stayed with the sick and so they did not *ibant* (go away) but still *ibant* (died). The verb is picked up in *obire* and then *subibant*.

1244 *pudor* is equivalent here to Thucydides' *aischyne* and is a powerful motive force in Greek and Roman literature: cf. Homer, *Iliad* 6. 442.

1245 Once again an idea from Thucydides is transformed into a deft sketch of a wretched scene. *blanda lassorum uox* well evokes the pleading voice of the exhausted – whether the patients or their tired relatives – and the polyptoton *uox...uoce* is a neat representation of the voice of pleading and the voice of lament mixed together. Where Thucydides had the relatives tired of 'making the ritual laments', Lucretius has put the groaning and wheedling of the sick themselves.

1246 Lucretius has demonstrated that craven flight from the sick did not rescue people from death and has now presented the opposite end of the moral spectrum in the figure of 'the best people' (*optimus quisque*) dying 'this sort of death'.

1247-51 The lines which appear here in the manuscript make much better sense if placed at the very end of the poem, as first suggested by Bockemüller. They have accordingly been transposed in this edition, and notes on them appear after the note on 1286.

1252-86 The migration into the city from the countryside and its results; Thucydides' account is as follows:

> Things were made even worse than they already were by the migration from the fields into the city, affecting the incoming folk especially. As there were no houses for them they had to live in

stifling huts in the summer season, and this produced a chaos of death, with dying corpses put on top of one another and half-dead people wallowing in the streets or grovelling around the springs in their thirst for water. The temples they camped out in were full of corpses who had died there on the spot. So overwhelming was the crisis that people turned to contempt for religion and divine law alike, not knowing what would become of them. All their old customs regarding the burial of the dead were disorganised and they buried the dead as each man could. So many people had already died that many people could not afford to bury properly and turned to disgraceful methods of disposal; some threw their own corpse onto an unlit pyre and set it alight, others threw the body they were carrying on top of an already blazing funeral pyre and then went home.   (2.52)

1252 The countryfolk are alluded to in increasingly epic terms: note the tricolon crescendo of: *pastor – armentarius omnis – robustus item...aratri*, and also the expressive epithet *robustus* which is ironic here as his strength will avail him little in the sick city and he quickly 'fainted' (*languebat*). Lucretius does not mention that these dying countryfolk have migrated into the city until lines 1259-61, but plunges *in medias res*.

1254 Note the accumulation of words denoting the idea of being 'pent-up' – *penitus, casa, contrusa* – and the way the line is framed by the two verbs conveying the idea of 'drooping'.

1255 The mention of 'poverty' is striking, as it suggests that Lucretius is asserting that their death was caused by poverty in the same way as it was caused by the disease; this is true in the sense that poverty allowed them less living space and so increased the chances of catching the disease from others.

1256-8 The most pathetic of all sights is that of parents and children dying together, their family unity emphasised in the near-repetition of *exanimis ...exanimata*; the misplaced *super* in 1258 shows the chaos of the heap of bodies. The sentence sets up a contrast which at first appears weak: sometimes (*nonnumquam*) you could see parents' corpses on top of their children's, sometimes you saw children's corpses on top of parents'. Its purpose is to force the reader to look longer at the scene of death and misery and to bring out the pathos of children dying before their parents (for which cf. Virgil, *Georgics* 4.476-7 (= *Aeneid* 6.307-8), Seneca, *ad Marciam* 1.2).

1259-61 The people of the countryside in Attica in fact came to live in the city of Athens to shelter behind the walls before the Spartan invasions, and

Lucretius assumes this knowledge on the part of the reader; otherwise the actions of sick countryfolk in moving to a sick city seem somewhat irrational.

1260 Note the sequence of *con-* words and the periphrasis *agricolarum copia* for 'a multitude of farmers' who were already *languens* – unlike the countrymen of Thucydides who caught the sickness in the city.

1261-2 The plethora is brought out by the twin statements that they came 'from all sides' and 'filled all places'. *loca* may mean 'open spaces' while *tecta* must mean 'buildings'.

1263 Note the personification of *mors* (for which, cf. 1273, 1242), also the emphasis on 'accumulation' in the verb (*accumulabat*), and the adverb (*aceruatim*).

1264 For the tmesis of *proque uoluta*, see 6.85, 230. There is a slight play on words as *strata* means 'streets' and is contained in *prostrata*, followed by *uiam* ('street').

1265 A *Silanus* was a fountain, presumably carved to look like the head of the appropriately bibulous satyr Silenus: cf. 4.1169 where the ugly girl with the snub nose is called *Silena*.

1266 Thucydides tells us that they 'grovelled round the springs in their thirst'; Lucretius adds the touch that they choked to death, drowned by their own thirst. There is tragic pathos in water that had 'all too much sweetness'.

1268 The poet gives an impressionistic picture of sick limbs 'with half-dead body' before supplying the descriptive adjectives in the next line.

1269 Note the chiasmus of *horrida paedore – pannis cooperta*, and the 'p' alliteration interlocking with 'c' alliteration in *pannis cooperta perire corporis*. Editors of this passage quote the 'old poet' whom Cicero cites (*Tusculan Disputations* 3.26) talking of how a 'beard shaggy with squalor (*paedore horrida*) and unshaven darkens his chest rough with filth'.

1270 The phrase 'only skin upon their bones' is a wholly new idea and continues the sequence of thought: they had rags on their bodies, with filth under the rags, and skin under the filth, and bones under the skin.

1271 The metaphorical use of *sepulta* ('buried' in ulcers) is grimly ironic in the light of the difficulties these corpses have in getting any proper burial after their death.

1272-5 Note the variation of vocabulary from *delubra* to *templa*, and again the personification of Death (as at 1263). *Mors* is appropriately placed among the bodies and the ubiquity of the dead is well brought out by the juxtaposition (in enjambement) of *passim/ cuncta*. There is also a faint mocking tone in the description of the 'temples of the heavenly gods' being 'loaded down' with corpses, breaking the taboo of death-free temples and the usual manner in which gods did not look on death; cf. Artemis' haughty leaving of the dying Hippolytus (Euripides, *Hippolytus* 1437-9, and see Barrett *ad loc.*). Lucretius regards all such taboos as irrational superstition.

1275 Another faintly comic touch: the temple-officials (*aedituentes* is only found here as alternative to the word *aeditui* and may be a mock-grandiose term for them) had filled the temple with 'guests'. Lucretius may mean that prior to the plague the temples had been filled with worshippers, in contrast to the impromptu morgues that the temples have now become, or he may intend a joke on the 'guests' who outstay their welcome by dying on their hosts.

1276-7 It is surprising that Lucretius did not make more of this point, in view of his trenchant hostility to *religio* in, for example, 1.62-101. The metaphor in *pendebantur* (cf. OLD s.v. 'pendo' 6b) is of being weighed in the balance and evaluated. Lucretius is perhaps playing on the original sense of *numina* as 'nodding of the head' to indicate divine will and suggests the nodding of the head as a tilting of the scales. After the long sentence *nec...enim* the brute reality of the pain is expressed in three words.

1279 *humare* means properly 'to bury', but both this passage and the Thucydidean source make it quite clear that cremation was carried out. OLD s.v. 'humo' 2 indicates that the verb may mean simply 'dispose of the dead' and that must be the meaning here.

1281 The line as transmitted in the manuscript is clearly incomplete. Of all the many emendations suggested, Housman's *propere pro tempore* has the double virtue of being the right sense and also palaeographically plausible. The whole phrase suggests the haste which *res subita* in the next line picks up, and the repetition of *pro-re* would easily be missed by a scribe.

1282 *multa* goes with *horrida* as the object of *suasit*: *res subita* as a phrase means 'emergency'. Poverty is relevant here in that the number of deaths (and therefore funerals) will have depleted their store of funeral expenses.

1283 The oxymoron of *consanguineos aliena* brings out the indecency of the act.

1284 The monstrous shout (*ingenti clamore*) could be the funeral lament or might refer forward to the brawling described in 1286. Notice Lucretius's painstaking description of the deed: the placing of the corpse itself (*locabant*) followed by the lighting of the pyre.

1285-6 The couplet has an awful irony about it: firstly, the living are injuring themselves in fighting over the dead; secondly their quarrels are futile as the dead themselves cannot feel or appreciate the efforts on their behalf (as proved in 3.830-1094). Finally there is an awful ambiguity about the 'massive bloodshed' present here: one associates bloodshed with death, only it is the living who are shedding each other's blood in actions which are pointless.

[1247-
51]   The lines as placed in the manuscript are usually printed with a lacuna indicated before them, but they make excellent sense here at the end of the poem.

[1247]   The living are attempting to bury the dead and all pretence of 'decent burial' seems lost. Note the polyptoton of *aliis alium* as the bodies are heaped up (cf. 1238) and the extravagant collective noun *populum* used to describe the 'masses' of their dead: if the plague produced the effect of genocide then the graves were inevitably mass graves.

[1248]   The struggle implied in *certantes* results in the fatigue of *lassi* and the whole experience produces the tears of grief (*lacrimis...luctu*), the line being heavily alliterative.

[1249]   These people are not actually sick, but they take to their beds out of grief as if they were.

[1250-1] The whole city was affected by suffering: notice the alliteration of *morbus ...mors* and then *temptaret tempore tali*. The poem ends on a sombre note of total desolation.